FINANCE AND ACCOUNTS
FOR MANAGERS

Also available in this series

Management Series

FINANCE AND ACCOUNTS FOR MANAGERS

DESMOND GOCH, F.A.C.C.A., A.M.B.I.M.

A PAN ORIGINAL

Revised and brought up to date

PAN BOOKS LTD : LONDON

First published 1969 by
PAN BOOKS LTD.,
33 Tothill Street, London, S.W.1

ISBN 0 330 02247 4

2nd (Revised) Printing 1971

Printed and bound in England by
Hazell Watson & Viney Ltd
Aylesbury, Bucks

Contents

Preface to Second Edition

In this second edition the chapter on Taxation (Chapter 21) has been revised and throughout the book decimal currency notation has been introduced into those examples affected by the change to the new monetary system.

DESMOND GOCH

Introduction

Many books have been written on the subject of accountancy – books for students preparing themselves for their professional examinations, books for qualified accountants who have to familiarize themselves with the latest developments within their particular specialism, and books for those non-accountants who are seeking to come to terms with the world of finance.

Why, then, yet another book about accountancy? This volume was conceived as one of a series on business management subjects that is being published in collaboration with the Editorial Advisory Board of the School of Business at Ealing Technical College. When the author was invited to contribute a book that would aim to explain the techniques of accountancy and their practical application to the solution of business management problems in terms which would be understood by managers who had received no formal training in business finance, it seemed to offer both a challenge and an opportunity to fill one of the remaining gaps in the wide range of accountancy literature.

From the author's own experience as an accountant in industry, many managers who are promoted from the ranks of their own specialism to accept wider responsibilities in a senior executive post, find that they are at a disadvantage when called upon to express opinions on matters of financial policy because of their lack of understanding of the basic principles of business finance.

No manager who aspires to direct the affairs of his company can afford to remain in ignorance of the financial aspects of its operations, or indeed of those of the industry or trade of which it forms a part, if only because at some stage of his career his own personal contribution to its trading fortunes will inevitably be assessed by yardsticks which are expressed in monetary terms. Because of the universality of accountancy in the context of business activity, the day when a manager could disclaim any interest in the financial affairs of his company is fast receding. He is now required to add numeracy to the forbidding list of attributes which are demanded of him if he is to win acceptance among his colleagues round the boardroom table.

This volume therefore sets out to explain in non-technical terms the wider background of accountancy and to relate it to the tasks which it has to perform. It starts with a brief outline of the historical developments which brought the art of accountancy from its humble origins as a residual skill of the merchant venturers of Venice to its present stature as the most important instrument of control in the management armoury. It goes on to examine the framework of company legislation on which has been built our present structure of modern industrial organization. The primary accounting documents, the balance sheet and the profit and loss account, are considered in their context as a record of stewardship of the management of shareholders' invested funds and as the financial scaffolding around which has been erected the edifice of management accounting techniques which are called in aid by the business executive who seeks to develop his expertise to its fullest extent.

Many of these techniques are long-established and

need little introduction to managers who are familiar with the financial disciplines of budgetary control and standard costing. Others, such as discounted cash flow, although they are not as new as many of their advocates would believe, are only now beginning to attract the attention of those managers who seek a sounder base on which to build their forecasts of the probable future trend of financial and economic events.

It is inevitable that some space has to be devoted to discussing some of the more mundane aspects of accountancy theory and practice, without, however, resorting to the minutiae of the double-entry book-keeping system. Indeed, when setting out to write this book, the author deliberately eschewed the notion that it is necessary to have a knowledge of the double-entry system if one is to understand what balance sheets and profit and loss accounts are all about. Many financial journalists and investment analysts provide the living proof that just as one does not need to be a playwright to become a competent and respected dramatic critic, so one does not need to be a qualified accountant to understand the basic elements of company accounts.

For all the very great value which can be derived from the use of management accountancy techniques, it is important to realize the limitations as well as the virtues which attach to them. The conventional balance sheet and profit and loss account are essentially historical documents, with all the disadvantages which that implies, and thus they cannot be expected to provide a reliable guide to future performance. The fact that a business has shown steady financial progress over a period of years does not ensure that it will continue to behave in the same way in the immediate future. To some extent the accountant's skill in advising on forward planning procedures may help to pierce the mist which cloaks future trading prospects, but he is no more skilful than the next man at manipulating a crystal ball.

Similarly, the balance sheet is largely a record of past spending and gives little, if any, indication of the current value of the business or of its underlying assets as represented by its buildings, plant and goodwill. Neither does one find in the balance sheet the capitalized value of such valuable assets as a vigorous management team and a skilled labour force – without which many businesses would be worth little more than the paper on which their balance sheets are printed. All this, the author hopes, will become apparent in due course to the reader of this book.

However, when proper allowance has been made for these limitations, there remains much in the accounts that can be of invaluable assistance to the business manager and it is the author's hope that this volume will make a genuine contribution to the better understanding of a subject which is intrinsically unexciting but which has so much to offer to those who have taken the trouble to find out what accountancy is all about.

DESMOND GOCH

CHAPTER ONE

The Accounting Scene

Although the use of financial control techniques as an
aid to managers in their task of running complex business operations has become accepted practice only
within the past thirty years or so, the application of
accountancy methods to the problems of recording commercial transactions can be traced back to the fifteenth
century in circumstances that are of considerable historical interest. Indeed, many of these early books of
accounts have themselves proved to be a valuable
source of information about the trading practices and
customs of their time.

Modern systems of accounting may seem very remote
from the era of parchment and quill pens, but the underlying principles owe something to the writings of a
Renaissance scholar, Luca Pacioli, who published his
*Summa de Arithmetica Geometria Proportione & Proportion-
alita* in Venice in 1494. Pacioli, a professor of mathematics at several Italian universities and a close friend
of Leonardo da Vinci, did not claim to have invented
the 'double entry' system of book-keeping – he was, he
said, merely recording the 'method of Venice': the
'Italian' system as it was sometimes known by the
merchants of that time.

The influence of his writings spread throughout
Europe and the first English textbook was published in

1543*, but it is a curious incident of accounting history that Scotland, which is widely acknowledged to be the cradle of modern accountancy, did not produce a work on double entry book-keeping until 1683†.

During the early years of this formative period the application of book-keeping methods was mainly confined to ecclesiastical, estate and local government records and to banking and merchanting transactions, but a body of knowledge was being developed which was to provide the foundations of the system of financial control that has now become an indispensable adjunct to managerial methods as we have come to apply them in the vastly different conditions of the present day.

The coming of the Industrial Revolution, with its demands for greatly increased investment in plant and machinery, necessitated the creation of business units of a size often beyond the capacity of a single individual to finance from his own resources, and this in turn was to lead to the evolution of the joint stock limited liability company. Raising capital from investors who were not involved at first hand nor required to participate in the day-to-day management of the business was not an easy operation unless some assurance could be given to them that they were not being asked to enter into an 'open ended' commitment. The concept of limited liability met this need and was undoubtedly a significant contributory factor in facilitating the expansion of the individual business unit – an expansion which was essential if the nation's economy was to be developed into that of a major industrial power.

* *A profitable Treatyce called the Instrument or Boke to learne to knowe the good order of the kepying of the famous reconynge called in Latyn, Dare and Habere, and in Englyshe, Debitor and Creditor.* Oldcastle, London, 1543.

† *Idea Rationaria,* or, *The Perfect accomptant.* Robert Colinson, Edinburgh, 1683.

Hand in hand with this increase in private investment in industry, came a demand for the managements of these new companies to give an account of their stewardship to the absentee owners – a demand that made calls on the skills of accountants and was in time to lead to a parallel growth in the memberships of the professional organizations that regulated their affairs. It was unfortunate, but perhaps inevitable, that this rise in commercial and industrial activity should bring about a corresponding rise in the number of bankruptcies and liquidations, and it was in this rather negative field of endeavour that many accountants came to make their living – specializing in winding up the affairs of those businesses that had failed to make a success of their trading ventures.

Even the introduction of income tax, albeit initially at a very low rate, made virtually no impact for many years on the accountancy profession and it contented itself with taking only a minor part in the early stages of the construction of the new industrial society which had begun to emerge.

A succession of financial scandals during the nineteenth century resulted in failures of public companies and forced the governments of the day to introduce increasingly stricter control of their activities by, among other measures, requiring them to submit to an annual audit of their accounts. This gave the accountancy profession an impetus to turn its attention to matters of a more constructive nature.

Despite this change of emphasis in its work, the nature of the auditing function meant that the accountancy profession maintained its obsessive interest in looking at the past. It was not until after the Second World War that a new generation of its members became imbued with the ideas propounded by a few pioneers who saw the need of industrial managements for a new approach based on the use of financial techniques as a positive instrument for controlling business activity. However, before considering the application of accountancy techniques and methods to the requirements of modern business, it is essential to appreciate why such a system is necessary.

Without a sophisticated monetary and credit system it would have been virtually impossible for the industrialized nations of the world to have reached their present advanced stage of development; accountancy has been the hand-maiden facilitating the achievement of these objectives.

Money performs several functions – it acts as a medium of exchange, as a store of value, as a claim on economic resources, and as a yardstick by which the relative values of dissimilar goods and services can be compared and measured. It is the universal medium which facilitates a civilized nation's economic existence, but it can be applied to these ends only if it is itself subjected to an element of discipline. Money which merely exists, without even the minor restraint of allowing itself to be counted, is of little use in the service of the community at large, and economic and business needs demand that it should be made to conform to some rather exacting rules.

Accountancy is, in fact, much more than just a means of disciplining money – its true function is to act as the language of business. If one accepts the premise that money is an indispensable adjunct to business activity, and it is difficult to admit otherwise, then it is easy to comprehend that most activities in business are eventually recorded in monetary terms – or at very least, their effect on total business activity will eventually be measurable, however indirectly, in the symbols that represent the pounds, shillings and pence of the monetary system.

ENTERPRISE NEEDS CAPITAL

Business enterprise cannot express itself in a tangible form without the investment of capital – in the case of a small concern the amount of capital may be quite modest and within the compass of one man's savings. With a large company, possibly the funds may have to come from the collective contributions of many hundreds of individual investors, but if they are to be successfully persuaded to subscribe their capital for the purposes set out in the prospectus or business plan, then they need to be assured that, so far as the nature of the enterprise permits, their funds will be secure and will earn a rate of interest that is commensurate with the degree of commercial risk involved.

It is only with the aid of accountancy techniques that these basic needs of the shareholder can be met – by producing financial statements that will show the sources from which the funds employed in the business have been raised and the uses to which they have been put, and how successfully they have been utilized in earning an appropriate rate of return by way of profit.

It is important to appreciate that despite the fact that the preparation of accounting statements requires technical expertise and skill, the accountant has to make assumptions which are often based on the personal opinions of experts in other fields – particularly in regard to such matters as the probable working life of plant, machinery and other equipment – and to this extent he is subject to the errors of human judgement. There is no absolute precision about accountancy and this point was very appositely made by a President of the American Institute of Certified Public Accountants when he said 'Few non-accountants understand, I fear, that precision in an income statement for a single year is unattainable'.*

The second respect in which accountancy techniques might be held to be deficient as a measuring instrument is their inability to place a monetary value on managerial skill and other forms of human talent. To the extent that the ability of its management has been the principal factor which has led a firm to commercial success, this will eventually be reflected in the rate of profit earned – but it may not be easy to say how much of this success is due to present managerial skill and effort, and how much is due to the sound decisions of earlier generations of managers.

But the fact remains that accountancy techniques provide business managements with a potent control system of unsurpassed effectiveness when used with reasonable competence and discrimination.

* Robert M. Trueblood speaking to a meeting of the Council of the American Institute of Certified Public Accountants on May 2nd, 1966.

CHAPTER TWO

Accountancy and the Legal Framework

Brief reference was made in the previous chapter to the tremendous increase in private investment in industry which followed the passage of legislation permitting and controlling the creation and operation of joint stock limited liability companies, and it is essential to a proper understanding of the application of accountancy techniques to the problems of business finance to have some knowledge of the various forms of legal constitution which govern business activity.

Prior to the introduction of legislation creating the concept of a corporate entity having a legal existence separate from that of its individual members, businesses were carried on either by a sole proprietor who accepted all the financial and legal risks as a personal responsibility, or by two or more persons combining to carry on their trading ventures as a joint partnership association.

Trading as a sole proprietor is not only the most elementary form of business organization but is also the one which normally carries the greatest individual financial risk. It is most suited to the small retail type of business where dealings are usually on a cash basis and the proprietor can devote most of his time to the day-to-day management of its affairs. In the event of a business failure the financial burden on the proprietor can be particularly heavy: the creditors are entitled to look to his private estate for satisfaction of their claims if the business assets are insufficient to pay them in full.

However, business ability and a ready supply of capital are not always concentrated in the same hands, so it is sometimes necessary for a venture to be undertaken jointly by forming a partnership association. Partnerships are a very common form of trading or professional organization, particularly when all the members are actively engaged in the daily management of the firm's affairs. As long as there is a strong degree of mutual trust and compatibility of temperament between the partners, such an association has many advantages – not least in the case of professional firms such as solicitors, accountants and stockbrokers.

For the normal type of commercial concern the partnership form of organization suffers from some of the defects that apply to a sole proprietorship. If the business fails, the private estates of the individual partners are liable to be taken in satisfaction of trade creditors' claims if the business assets are insufficient to meet the partnership liabilities. Furthermore, the admission of new partners and the retirement of existing ones sometimes creates problems of a nature which it is not always possible to anticipate by prior agreement.

But, in spite of these drawbacks, the partnership form of organization has the advantage of being fairly flexible as it is open to the individual members to make such rules as they wish without having to observe numerous legal restrictions of the type that apply to limited companies. The Partnership Act, 1890, makes provision for certain rules of conduct and procedure if the partners have not made a formal agreement governing their duties, rights and obligations, and there is at present a statutory restriction which limits them to twenty members*. As the taxation law stands at the present time, there are, too, certain tax advantages to be gained by trading in this way rather than as a limited company.

While the partnership form of association went some way towards meeting the need for concentrating capital and managerial resources into larger units, it was still inadequate to meet the ever-growing demands of industry in the period of rapid expansion which transformed Britain's economy in the nineteenth century.

The capital investment required to develop and exploit the new technologies of the Industrial Revolution outgrew the financial resources that could be gathered together within a partnership form of organization – depending as it did on a high degree of mutual trust and personal acquaintanceship to support the burden of financial risk that it entailed. The new industrial environment demanded a means of attracting fresh capital from many sources by methods which would ensure that individual investors could agree to the normal trading risks of business enterprise without being asked to accept an 'open ended' liability that would involve them in financial commitments far beyond the scale they could reasonably contemplate.

It was to meet this need for widening the basis for participation in the finance of new ventures that the concept of limited liability was born, and the outcome was to be the tapping of many new sources of investment capital and a corresponding broadening of the base of industrial ownership and risk-bearing.

The joint stock limited liability company is nowadays by far the most important form of business organization

* The Companies Act, 1967 abolished this restriction in the case of partnerships of solicitors, accountants and stockbrokers.

and also the one which is most closely circumscribed by legislative supervision and regulation.

It is based on the concept of a corporation having a legal existence separate from that of its individual members, and its application to trading firms had its origins in such famous corporations as the East India Company and the Hudson's Bay Company. However, these early trading companies were created by Royal Charter, a form of constitution which was obviously unsuited to the rapidly-expanding economy of the nineteenth century. The circumstances demanded a more flexible form of organization and the answer came with the passing of legislation that facilitated the creation of companies of a type similar in most respects to those which are nowadays incorporated under the provisions of the Companies Acts, 1948 and 1967.

The fundamental principle of limited liability is that the individual members subscribe to the company's capital by the purchase of its shares under the terms of this legislation and its own constitution – its Memorandum and Articles of Association. Once this share capital has been fully paid up by the members they have no further financial liability and are thereby protected from actions brought by the company's creditors against their personal estate in the event of its trading operations being unsuccessful and leading to its insolvency. As a consequence of its members' limited liability the company is obliged to include the word 'Limited' (abbreviated to Ltd) as the last word in its title, thereby warning those who trade with it that the members, unlike those of an unincorporated partnership, cannot be held to be personally liable for its debts.

From the investor's point of view this new form of trading organization overcame many of the disadvant-

ages of absentee proprietorship inherent in the partnership method of trading, and secure in the knowledge
that his private estate was not subject to sequestration
in the event of the company's failure, he was encouraged
to provide further capital to finance the many new
commercial ventures that were being inaugurated.

There were, of course, some abuses of these privileges,
but over the years a succession of Companies Acts,
culminating in the Acts of 1948 and 1967, have modern-
ized the procedures and tightened the supervision over
company affairs nowadays entrusted to the Registrar of
Companies acting as a department of the Board of
Trade.

THE COMPANY CONSTITUTION

Two distinct categories of companies are permitted by
the Companies Acts. Firstly, private companies – those
companies which by their constitution restrict the
right to transfer their shares and limit the number of
members to a maximum of fifty – and secondly, public
companies, being those which do not carry these
restrictions.

Companies that apply for a stock exchange quotation
so that their shares may be bought and sold through the
stock market mechanism must, of course, come into the
latter category, and in the case of those that make their
application to the London Stock Exchange, they must
comply with the detailed regulations enforced by its
Quotations Department.

Subject to the broad limitations of the Companies
Acts, the promoters of a company can make their own
rules for the regulation of its internal affairs and they are
set out in its Memorandum and Articles of Association.

These two documents define its broad trading objectives, authorized capital, voting rights of members, appointment of directors, borrowing powers, and the numerous other matters which need to be defined if it is to be governed in a constitutional manner.

One of the most important aspects of a company's legal existence is the rights that attach to its share capital and the principal characteristics of the more common types of shares are summarized below:

Preference Shares. These shares usually carry the right to a fixed rate of dividend that may accumulate from one year to the next in the event of there being insufficient profits to meet the payment. If the company is put into liquidation, the holder's right to a return of capital is normally confined to the nominal (or face) value of the share.

It is usually the case that preference shares carry no voting rights, or possibly limited rights which become effective if the dividend remains unpaid in any year.

Ordinary Shares. A company's ordinary share capital is often referred to as the 'equity' of the business – a term which reflects the position of the ordinary shareholders as the ultimate risk-bearers and owners of the residual capital.

This type of share normally carries no entitlement to a fixed rate of dividend, ranking in this respect behind any preference shares which are in issue, and its holder is dependent on the profitability of the business for the amount he receives by way of return on his investment. On the other hand, because of his right to participate in the residue of profit which remains after the prior interests have been met, he may enjoy a high rate of return if the company is particularly successful.

Ordinary shares usually carry superior voting rights and in the event of the company being put into liquidation the holders are entitled to any surplus capital funds that remain after all prior claims have been met.

Other types of shares carrying special dividend and voting rights are often met with in practice but they generally have some of the principal characteristics of either preference or ordinary shares.

Debentures and Loan Stock. Some companies may decide to raise a part of their capital requirements in forms other than that of permanent share capital, depending on the nature and time span of the projects they are seeking to finance. Such funds are normally raised by way of an issue of debentures or loan stock – the capital being subscribed in the form of a fixed interest loan rather than as a variable dividend direct stake in the business. Loan capital is very often borrowed for a fixed period of time (five, ten or twenty years) and the lenders may be assured of the security of their funds by granting them a charge on the company's fixed assets.

PROTECTION FOR THE INVESTOR

Successive Companies Acts have strengthened those regulations which have been designed to safeguard the position of investors, and more particularly the rules relating to prospectuses and accounts, but no record of the advances made in company legislation would be complete without mentioning the pioneering work of the Council of the London Stock Exchange.

The most important advance in recent times has undoubtedly been the passing of the Companies Act, 1967, which introduced important provisions dealing with the disclosure of information in published accounts, and it represented the culmination of a gradual change in the climate of opinion favouring an extension of the limits to which boards of directors were prepared to go by voluntary action in advance of new legislation.

Regarding such matters as the disclosure of turnover figures and profits arising from the principal trading activities, the real break-through came when the Council of the London Stock Exchange anticipated this legislation by several years when it introduced new rules which required companies coming to the market for additional capital to give this information in their accounts on a regular basis.

Prospectuses. When a public company seeks to raise capital by an issue of share capital or loan stock, it is required to publish a prospectus that contains a considerable amount of information about its past history and future prospects, primarily of a financial and legal nature, and this document becomes the basis of the offer that the subscribing investor is deemed to have accepted.

Accounts. All companies, public and private, are required to submit to their members an annual directors' report and accounts giving at least the minimum amount of information demanded by the Companies Acts, 1948 and 1967, but in practice many companies give supplementary financial and statistical material that goes far towards satisfying the most inquisitive shareholder.

However, even more important from the point of view of ensuring that the accounts give a true and fair view of the company's financial and trading position is the requirement that the books and accounts should be subject to annual audit by a firm of auditors whose members belong to a body of professional accountants recognized for this purpose by the Board of Trade. Although the first appointment of auditors is usually brought about as a result of approaches made to them by the board of directors, they are in fact responsible directly to the members and have the right to attend the company's annual general meeting and, under certain circumstances, to make representations direct to them.

Large companies that trade extensively on a national or international scale frequently organize their financial and administrative structure so that the various activities are carried on through subsidiary companies – either wholly or partly owned – but with this method of operation it is not easy for shareholders to appreciate the overall financial position merely by studying the accounts of the parent (or holding) company. The Companies Act, 1948, met this situation by introducing a requirement that holding companies should present to their shareholders a consolidated balance sheet and profit and loss account which combine the assets, liabilities and trading results of the parent company with those of all its subsidiaries, thereby presenting an overall view of the group financial position which it would not be possible to obtain from the conventional accounts.

The legislation governing the constitution and administration of joint stock companies is lengthy and complex but it is an inevitable corollary of the widening spread of ownership of industry.

CHAPTER THREE

The Money in the Business

From the shareholder's point of view, the principal requirement of an accounting system is to show the sources from which the company's capital funds have been derived and the uses to which they have been put, and then to measure and report on the degree of success that has been achieved in earning the income which arises from their application to particular trading or commercial activities.

The first aspect of this function of accounting for the stewardship of funds is reflected in the Balance Sheet – a financial statement which shows on the one hand the sources from which the company's capital has been derived – issues of share capital, long term loans, retained profits, etc – and, on the other hand, the various ways in which these monetary resources are deployed – the purchase of plant, machinery, stocks of raw materials, or as cash retained in the bank.

This dual aspect of a balance sheet can best be explained by taking the simple example of a new company that has been formed with an issued and paid up share capital of £100 in units of £1 Ordinary Shares and which has used the funds thus raised to buy a machine and a stock of raw materials with which to carry on its manufacturing activities. Assuming that the machine cost £40 and £50 was spent on trading stocks, the balance sheet at this date would appear as follows:

BALANCE SHEET

Share Capital		£	Assets	£
100 £1 Ordinary Shares			Machine at cost	40
Issued and fully paid	100		Stock of materials	50
			Cash at bank	10
	100			100

It will be seen from this very elementary balance sheet that it is a statement of the capital funds employed, showing both the sources and the dispositions of the funds which have been invested at that date, and in some respects can be likened to a financial snapshot of the company's position at that particular point in time.

The capital funds employed in the business of an established company will, of course, be derived from a number of sources – its long term financing requirements being met by issues of Preference or Ordinary shares, possibly augmented by loans raised in the form of loan stock for a specified period of time at a fixed rate of interest, with supplementary needs being met by retaining a part of each year's trading profits after adequate dividends have been distributed to the shareholders. The fluctuating short term needs of the business will be met by the use of temporary borrowing facilities such as are normally provided by bank loans and overdrafts, and even more transient will be the short term capital which comes from the credit allowed by suppliers who have provided materials or services on monthly account terms.

On the opposite side of the balance sheet, in addition to the amounts expended on the acquisition of capital assets such as buildings, plant, machinery, etc, there will be shown the amount of the working capital funds which, depending on the nature of the business, have been employed in the purchase and holding of trading stocks pending their resale or conversion by manufacturing processes into finished products.

The way in which these many different kinds of financial transactions are reflected in a company's accounts will now be considered in relation to the balance sheet of an imaginary company (see page 51).

Share Capital. Looking first at the Capital Employed section of this balance sheet, it will be seen that the company has raised a substantial part of its permanent capital requirement by an issue of 200,000 7% £1 Preference Shares which produced a total of £200,000, and 600,000 £1 Ordinary Shares to bring in a further £600,000. In regard to the Ordinary Shares, it should be explained that although they are stated to have a value of £1 each, this is only a nominal value which attaches in compliance with the requirements of the Companies Acts and does not represent the prospective marketable value. Once a company has made its initial issue of share capital and has commenced trading, then any further issues of shares would almost certainly be at a price which is fixed by reference to its subsequent profits record.

When a later issue of shares has been made at a price above their stated nominal value, the proceeds must be shown in the balance sheet in a manner which distinguishes between the nominal value and the premium element. Thus, if a company makes an issue of 100,000 £1 Ordinary Shares at a price of £1·25 each, the proceeds would be shown in its balance sheet as to £100,000 in the Ordinary Share Capital account and £25,000 (the £0·25 per share premium) in the Share Premium account. It is necessary to segregate the premium element in this way so as to comply with the requirements of the Companies Acts, but for all practical purposes there is no fundamental distinction between the nominal value and premium elements. In the case of the specimen balance sheet which is now being considered, it will be seen that the proceeds of the issue of Ordinary Shares has produced a total of £650,000, of which £50,000 represents the premium and is accordingly shown in a Share Premium Account.

Reserves. Immediately following the share capital and share premium accounts there is shown a General Reserve of £275,000 and a balance of £45,000 on the Profit and Loss Account, the total sum of £320,000 representing the amount of trading profits which, after providing for taxation and dividend payments, has been retained in the business to provide additional funds for future development. The practice of transferring a part of the balance on the Profit and Loss Account to a specific reserve (in this case the General Reserve) is largely a matter of accountancy presentation, often resorted to so as to emphasize the fact that such sums are to be regarded as having been 'ploughed back' into the business rather than being available for distribution by way of dividends. If a company has built up a considerable balance of retained profits in this way, the directors sometimes recommend to the shareholders that the permanent retention of funds should be recognized in a more positive manner by capitalizing a portion of such reserves. This is in essence a book-keeping transaction that entails transferring a part of the balance on the reserve account up to the Share Capital account by the

creation of additional shares which are then issued as
fully paid up capital to the existing members propor-
tionately to their present holdings.

Such a transaction is of relatively little significance in
regard to the disposition of funds within the business and
its principal purpose is to emphasize that the amounts so
capitalized are no longer to be considered as available
for dividend payments. Share capital, even when
created in this way, cannot be repaid to the shareholders except at the conclusion of a winding up of the
company's activities after all the creditors' claims have
been met, or by a partial return of capital under a re-
construction scheme which has been approved by the
Court.

Where a capitalization issue of this nature has been
made for the purpose of bringing the nominal share
capital more closely into line with the total of members'
capital employed in the business, it has the further
advantage of enabling dividend payments to be more
accurately expressed in relation to the total funds which
are represented thereby. The present practice in the
United Kingdom is for dividend payments to be expressed as a percentage of the nominal value of the
share capital, without regard to any other capital employed as represented by retained profits which have
been put to revenue reserves.

Taking the example of the specimen balance sheet
(see page 52), the directors may be assumed to have declared a dividend of 15 per cent on the Ordinary Share
capital and this will be calculated as a percentage of the
nominal value of £600,000 – the total cost of the
Ordinary Dividend therefore being £90,000. However,
when this rate of return on capital is related not just to
the nominal value of the Ordinary Shares, but also to

the additional capital funds represented in the balance sheet by the Share Premium Account (£50,000), the General Reserve (£275,000) and the balance on the Profit and Loss Account (£45,000), it will be seen that the total of the funds which derive from the Ordinary Shareholders' investment is as follows:

	£
600,000 Ordinary Shares of £1 each	600,000
Capital Reserve – Share Premium Account	50,000
General Reserve	275,000
Profit and Loss Account	45,000
Total Ordinary Shareholders' funds	970,000

Thus, when the proposed dividend of 15 per cent on the nominal share capital is expressed as a percentage of the total Ordinary Shareholders' funds, the true rate of return is £90,000/£970,000, ie 9·3 per cent.

It is apparent that the practice of expressing dividends as a percentage of the nominal value of the share capital rather than as a proportion of the total capital attributable to the ordinary shareholders can give a misleading impression of the rate of dividend being distributed.

Because the capitalization of undistributed profits by a transfer from reserves to share capital does bring about a reduction of the gap between nominal capital and the total funds employed, it goes some way towards overcoming the disadvantages inherent in the present method of expressing dividends. Using the previous example, if it is assumed that the directors have decided to carry out such a capitalization operation by taking £150,000 from the General Reserve and utilizing the balance of £50,000 on the Share Premium Account, the total sum of £200,000 being transferred to the

Ordinary Share capital account by issuing shares on the basis of one new share for every three held, the relevant part of the balance sheet would be shown as follows:

CAPITAL EMPLOYED

	£	£
Share Capital – Authorized and Issued		
200,000 7% Preference Shares – £1 ea. fully paid		200,000
800,000 Ordinary Shares – £1 ea. fully paid		800,000
		1,000,000
Reserves		
Revenue – General Reserve	125,000	
– Profit and Loss Account	45,000	
		170,000
		1,170,000

It will be seen that the total of the Ordinary Shareholders' funds invested in the business remains at £970,000 (Share Capital £800,000 and Reserves £170,000), but whereas a dividend declared at the rate of 10 per cent on the new share capital would require a sum of £80,000, this now represents a rate of 8·25 per cent on the Ordinary Shareholders' funds. By making a capitalization issue by transfers from reserves, the gap between the percentage rates expressed on the two bases has been considerably narrowed, although not, of course, completely eliminated.

Loan Stock. Returning again to the specimen balance sheet, the next item is 6% Unsecured Loan Stock 1975–1980 – £250,000. Raising new capital requirements by an issue of loan stock (or by the creation of a debenture) is an alternative to issuing additional share capital, but there is a material distinction in the legal relationship that exists between the company and these two classes of investors.

Whereas a shareholder is a member of the company and, depending on the rights which attach to his class of shares, may have voting rights which can be exercised at its general meetings, a loan stockholder has no such status and is nearer to being a simple lender of funds who has special rights which he can exercise in particular circumstances.

An issue of loan stock carries a fixed rate of interest which is payable whether or not the company is earning profits and the security for the capital debt is frequently enhanced by the creation of a prior charge exercisable on specific assets. Such a charge ensures that in the event of the company going into liquidation the assets thus secured are available in the first instance to meet the repayment of capital to the loan stockholders, ranking in priority to trade creditors and shareholders. Conversely, they have no right to participate in surplus profits or capital beyond their predetermined entitlement.

Loan stock issues are often preferred as the method of capitalization when funds are required to finance a project over a fixed period of years, and provision is normally made for the capital to be repaid at the end of a specified period (between 1975 and 1980 in the case of the company represented by the specimen balance sheet). The funds for repayment are usually provided by annual appropriations from the profits arising on the project which is being financed or by the proceeds of a further issue of loan stock or share capital.

Other considerations will arise when deciding on the

method of capitalization to be adopted and these will
be dealt with in a later chapter, but mention should be
made that taxation legislation will often be a material
factor when the advantages and disadvantages of the
various methods of raising capital are being weighed
in the balance.

Deferred Taxation. In 1965 a new system of taxing company profits was introduced and the former two-tier
system of Income Tax and Profits Tax was replaced by
the single-tier Corporation Tax. Under the new system
the time-lag that existed between the earning of profits
and the payment of the tax thereon was considerably
reduced, but even now the length of the period of delay
will vary according to the date on which a company
ends its financial year.

Our imaginary company, with a financial year that
ends on December 31st, does not have to pay its tax on
trading profits until January 1st twelve months hence
and is therefore able to retain the funds in the business
until they are required to meet the liability when it
becomes due. Because of its deferred nature, some
companies show this item separately in the balance
sheet under an appropriate heading such as 'Deferred
Taxation', whereas others prefer to include it under the
general heading of Current Liabilities.

CHAPTER FOUR

Employing the Capital – I

Depending on the nature of the company's business, it will use some of its capital funds for the purpose of acquiring the buildings, plant, machinery, motor vehicles and equipment (known in accounting language by the generic term 'fixed assets') which it needs for the purpose of carrying on its trading activities, and the amount of capital so expended is shown in the balance sheet under the appropriate general category headings.

However, the fixed assets that are represented by this expenditure do not normally have an indefinite working life; their useful life-span may vary from three or four years in the case of some motor vehicles to upwards of fifty years for factory and office buildings – and in the case of leasehold premises their accounting life will obviously coincide with the period of the lease.

Quite clearly, it would not give a fair picture of a company's trading results if the cost of acquiring these various fixed assets were to be charged wholly against the trading income of the year in which they were first purchased, as these years would thereby be burdened with costs which bore no relationship to the success or otherwise of the company's normal trading activities and subsequent years would escape their fair share of capital charges. Accounting practice therefore requires that the cost of acquiring these capital assets should be spread over a period of years which corresponds with their estimated useful working life. Thus, if a machine were to be bought at a cost of £10,000 and it had an estimated working life of ten years, the original expenditure would be recorded in the appropriate fixed asset account and would then be written off as a charge against the trading results of the next ten years by equal annual amounts of £1,000.

The accounting process of writing off capital expenditure over a period of years in this way entails making an annual charge to the profit and loss account for depreciation of fixed assets and carrying forward the unexpired portion of original cost under the appropriate fixed asset heading in the balance sheet.

In the case of the machine quoted in the example above, at the end of the first year of its working life it would appear in the balance sheet as follows:

	£
Plant and machinery at cost	10,000
Less: Depreciation to date	1,000
Net book value	9,000

By the end of the tenth year the full cost will have been charged against revenue and the book cost of the asset will no longer appear in the balance sheet. If the original estimate of the machine's useful working life was accurate, the final annual 'write off' will coincide with its withdrawal from operational use.

Although this method of spreading the cost of capital expenditure over a period of years ensures that no one trading period bears a disproportionate part of the burden, it is important to appreciate that the actual cash outlay is normally made in the first year and only the charging of this cost against revenue is deferred to later years.

Thus, the act of incurring capital expenditure, unless it is financed by leasing or hire purchase arrangements, results in an immediate depletion of cash resources which is only made good over a period of time as the annual charges for depreciation provide for the retention of an equivalent amount of cash, until by the time the asset has been finally written off the original cash outflow will have been fully recovered.

FIXED ASSET VALUES

The conventional accounting treatment of expenditure on fixed assets is undoubtedly widely misunderstood by many businessmen who are not familiar with practice in this respect and it is a source of confusion to laymen when they are trying to come to terms with balance sheets and profit and loss accounts. They frequently, but erroneously, gain the impression that the book values at which these assets are shown in the balance sheet can be related to the realizable value that would be produced if they were to be disposed of piecemeal or as part of a going concern.

It cannot be too strongly emphasized that the vast majority of companies prepare their accounts on the basis of recording historical costs, and their balance sheets must therefore be regarded as accounts of stewardship showing the sources of capital funds and the uses to which they have been put rather than as a statement of the present capital value of the business as a going concern. A small minority of companies (including some of the largest in the country) do, in fact, provide for their fixed assets to be revalued from time to time and in some cases these revised values are incorporated in their balance sheets, but this practice is still very much the exception to the rule.

Over the past twenty years or so, many accountants and economists have questioned the adequacy of conventional accounting practice under the conditions of sustained monetary inflation which have prevailed throughout this period. The orthodox method of accounting admirably fulfils its purpose of maintaining the shareholders' capital intact for so long as the principal monetary unit maintains a constant purchasing power, but with the persistent erosion of the value of the pound sterling over the past thirty years the validity of these techniques has been seriously challenged.

These criticisms are particularly relevant in regard to the problem of financing the cost of replacing fixed assets which have reached the end of their useful working life. It will have been seen from the earlier explanation of the method of amortizing the cost of fixed assets by annual depreciation charges against revenue over their estimated working life that cash resources are thereby restored to their original level by the time the expenditure has been fully written off, but while these funds are now available to finance further investment in fixed assets, the cost of providing similar equipment will in the meantime undoubtedly have shown a marked increase because of the general upward movements in most price levels.

In the case of companies which have to maintain a high level of investment in capital equipment, the problems of plant replacement can place a considerable strain on cash resources – particularly when a re-equipment programme has to be mounted over a short period of time.

A variety of proposals have been put forward to deal with this situation and among the most favoured suggestions is the periodic revaluation of the existing fixed assets so as to bring their book values into line with current price levels. By introducing these enhanced values into the balance sheet and thereby basing the annual depreciation charge on the new figures, additional cash resources will be retained within the business and thus be available to meet the extra cost of replacement when it has to be faced.

Comparatively few companies have grasped this particular nettle and to the extent that they have elected to recognize this problem at all, most of them have confined their action to setting aside out of their annual trading profits such sums as are estimated to be required as a provision for the future replacement of capital equipment.

Goodwill, Patents and Trade Marks. In addition to using their capital funds for the purchase of fixed assets such as plant and machinery, many companies that are seeking to expand their business pay substantial sums to acquire the right to use trade marks or patents that are likely to give them access to new trade outlets.

Sums expended in this way do in fact result in the acquisition of valuable assets, albeit of an intangible nature, and in the normal course of events it can be expected that the benefits which accrue from their exploitation will be reflected in future trading profits. In some respects, therefore, this type of capital expenditure can be treated in the accounts in much the same way as that which is incurred on the purchase of physical assets such as buildings and plant, with the cost being

The 1948 Act introduced new regulations requiring parent companies to prepare group accounts consisting of a consolidated balance sheet and profit and loss account embodying the combined assets and liabilities and profits or losses of all the companies within the group. These consolidated accounts also show the extent to which any outside shareholders are interested in the capital, reserves and profits of the subsidiaries and thus give the parent company's shareholders a more realistic picture of the disposition of their invested funds.

For practical purposes a subsidiary company is defined as being one in which the parent company holds more than one half of the ordinary share capital.

Other Shareholdings. In addition to investments held in subsidiary companies, companies sometimes take up a shareholding interest in firms with which they have a trade connection, but restrict their investment so as to constitute only a minority proportion of the total share capital. There are many reasons as to why a company might decide to limit its financial interest in this way, but very often a substantial minority interest is quite sufficient to achieve a degree of control without going to the length of a full take-over.

Where a company has taken up a shareholding interest of this nature there is, of course, no requirement to include the associated company's assets and liabilities in the group consolidated accounts. Instead, it is sufficient to show the amount of capital so invested under the general heading of Investments as in the specimen balance sheet on page 51 – distinguishing where necessary between quoted and unquoted investments.

With the passing of the Companies Act, 1967, new regulations have been enacted extending the statutory requirements regarding disclosure of information relating to investments held in other companies and in future the range of financial detail in this respect will be very much extended.

CHAPTER FIVE

Employing the Capital – II

In addition to the funds invested in the buildings, plant, machinery and other fixed assets, which are required to carry on the company's activities, it will also be necessary for the shareholders to make available further funds to finance the business's working capital requirements.

During the period of time which elapses between the commencement of work on a customer's order and the receipt of cash in final settlement of his account (this may be anything from six weeks or more after delivery has been completed), the business has to finance from its own resources the purchase of materials and bought-in components, wages, salaries, and other overheads. This represents a permanent commitment of working capital because the business must always expect to be without some of its potential cash resources: they will be tied up in work in progress and in the form of debts owed by customers whose period of credit has not yet expired.

Conversely, the company can in turn expect that its own suppliers will grant a similar period of credit and to this extent it will gain a permanent short term addition to its total working capital resources.

In the specimen balance sheet (see page 51) it will be seen that the company has an amount of £1,215,000 invested in current assets and owes a total of £795,000 in respect of current liabilities – thus showing net working capital of £420,000. When assessing a business's working capital position, it is essential to appreciate the nature of the items which are customarily included under the general heading of current assets.

STOCK AND WORK IN PROGRESS

The nature and value of the trading stock and work in progress, which are brought into the inventory when the physical stock count is made at the close of the financial year, are of particular importance in this respect. The significance for accounting purposes of the closing stock and work in progress in relation to the ascertainment of the year's trading profit is explained in the next chapter and the valuation aspects are dealt with in Chapter 18. But it is essential to the proper understanding of a balance sheet to appreciate that, in addition to representing the value of the working capital resources which are employed at the balance sheet date, it also shows the value of the expenditure on materials incurred in the year under review which has been carried forward as a charge against the revenue of the next trading period.

Although trading stocks are customarily valued at cost or market value, whichever is lower, the valuation is based on the over-riding assumption that the business is to be viewed as a continuing entity and that the individual stock items which comprise the closing inventory will realize the value placed on them for this purpose when they eventually come to be sold in a subsequent trading period. Indeed, unless the annual accounts are prepared on this basis it would be impossible to ascertain a commercially realistic figure of trading profit (or loss) for the period.

The extent to which the individual company needs to

commit a part of its working capital resources in the financing of stock and work in progress will obviously depend on the nature of its business activities. Thus, a company that confines itself to the provision of service facilities (such as office cleaning or equipment maintenance) will probably require only a small amount of capital investment in the form of materials stocks. At the other extreme a firm of shipbuilders or aircraft manufacturers would have to invest considerable sums of money in the form of materials, wages, salaries, and overhead expenditure during the lengthy period which will elapse between the time when work on a project is first started and the eventual delivery of the ship or aircraft to the operator. To some extent, of course, the problem of financing work in progress on contract work of this nature is alleviated by the practice of requiring progress payments, but the nature of the business will still entail a considerable commitment of resources.

Although for the purposes of accounting presentation the total value of the capital resources which are employed in this way is customarily shown under the general heading of Current Assets (this being expenditure on assets which will eventually emerge at the end of the production/sales cycle in the form of cash), in the short term it cannot be regarded as a part of the immediate liquid or near-liquid funds that are available to meet maturing liabilities.

DEBTORS

When work in progress has eventually been converted into finished goods, it has obviously become very much nearer to fitting the description of 'current assets', although even then, unless the items concerned are due

for delivery, there may be a further period of immobiliza-
tion of working capital until they are despatched from
the warehouse and invoiced to the customer.

The item 'Debtors – £635,000' in the specimen
balance sheet represents, in broad terms, those customer
accounts that at the balance sheet date were still unpaid. Some of the individual accounts included in this
figure will refer to deliveries made in the last months of
the financial year and in those cases where the goods
have been supplied on customary monthly account
terms they will not yet be due for settlement. But, in the
normal course of events, not every customer adheres
strictly to monthly payments and it is usual to find that
a proportion of the total sum owed by trade debtors
will represent overdue accounts. The problems that may
be encountered as the result of slow payment of accounts are referred to in detail in Chapter 17.

CREDITORS

Just as the normal custom of trade frequently requires
that customers shall be granted a period of grace before
they are required to settle their accounts, so the company's own suppliers will in turn extend a similar period
of credit in respect of its purchases of raw materials,
components and services, etc, and thus it will obtain
the benefit of a temporary addition to its working
capital resources. The item 'Creditors – £508,000'
represents the value of those accounts which have been
accepted by the company but which had not been paid
at the balance sheet date.

BANK OVERDRAFT

It will be seen from the specimen balance sheet that the company had a bank overdraft of £135,000 at the close of its financial year but it must be emphasized that this will not necessarily represent the full extent of its credit facility from this source.

Many companies rely on the short term credit facilities provided by their bankers to enable them to cover their day-to-day commitments while they are awaiting the monthly inflow of cash from their customers. Others, who operate in industries with a trading pattern of a highly seasonal nature, will require similar accommodation while awaiting the cash receipts from their peak-season sales.

Credit facilities of this nature are usually subject to annual review by the company's bankers although they often come to be regarded as a semi-permanent source of short-term working capital. Indeed, although bank overdrafts are theoretically repayable on demand, in practice it might be very difficult for a business to comply with such a request at short notice.

Because many firms will normally seek to work within the credit limit which they have negotiated with their bankers, it may well be that their potential facilities are in excess of their actual borrowings at the balance sheet date.

TAXATION AND DIVIDENDS

The items 'Current Taxation – £48,000' and 'Proposed Dividends – £104,000' represent maturing commitments which will have to be discharged within a short period of the balance sheet date.

TREASURY BILLS AND
TAX RESERVE CERTIFICATES

Even though the company may be utilizing its bank credit facilities for its day-to-day working capital requirements, the need may arise to set aside funds to meet forthcoming commitments such as the payment of tax or incurring capital expenditure on acquiring new plant.

Treasury Bills are but one of a number of possible ways of investing cash funds that are temporarily surplus to working capital needs or that have to be specifically earmarked. They have the advantage that they can quickly be converted into cash, although they are normally purchased to mature at a specific date within their three months term.

Although the division between fixed and working capital is usually self-evident, it must be remembered that a balance sheet is essentially a static document which portrays the sources and dispositions of the capital employed in the business at a particular moment in time. While movements within the fixed capital part of the structure may not be rapid, the working capital element is undergoing a process of constant change and a lapse of 24 hours may well show a considerable variation in the composition of the various items. The many problems associated with the control of fixed and working capital resources are dealt with in later chapters of this book.

Balance Sheet at December 31st, 197–

EMPLOYMENT OF CAPITAL

	Cost £	Depreciation £	Net £
Fixed Assets			
Freehold Premises	410,000	65,000	345,000
Plant and Machinery	590,000	185,000	405,000
Motor Vehicles	45,000	20,000	25,000
	1,045,000	270,000	775,000
Goodwill, Patents and Trade Marks			110,000
Investments			
Subsidiary Company		125,000	
Quoted Investments (market value £45,000)		40,000	
Unquoted Investments		25,000	
			190,000
Current Assets			
Stock and Work in Progress		540,000	
Debtors		635,000	
Treasury Bills		15,000	
Tax Reserve Certificates		25,000	
		1,215,000	
Current Liabilities			
Creditors		508,000	
Bank Overdraft		135,000	
Current Taxation		48,000	
Proposed Dividends		104,000	
		795,000	
Net Current Assets			420,000
			£1,495,000

Balance Sheet at December 31st, 197– *(continued)*

CAPITAL EMPLOYED	£	£
Share Capital – Authorized and Issued		
200,000 7% Preference Shares £1 ea. fully paid		200,000
600,000 Ordinary Shares £1 ea. fully paid		600,000
Reserves		
Capital – Share Premium Account		50,000
Revenue – General Reserve	275,000	
– Profit and Loss Account	45,000	
		320,000
		1,170,000
6% *Unsecured Loan Stock* 1975–1980		250,000
Deferred Taxation		
Corporation Tax payable January 1st, 197–		75,000
		£1,495,000

CHAPTER SIX

The Profit and Loss Account

We must now consider the other major aspect of financial reporting – that which concerns itself with measuring the profit which accrues from the employment of the capital resources that have been dealt with in the preceding chapters.

The ascertainment of trading profit is essentially the matching of costs against revenue – apportioning expenditure and income against the accounting periods to which they relate – and the resulting surplus (if any), after provision has been made for taxation, represents the net return on the capital resources employed which can be considered as available to meet shareholders' dividend requirements.

However, while the application of accountancy techniques to the determination of business profits entails the observance of certain widely-accepted principles, it is not a precise science and depends to a very great extent on the personal judgement of those who are responsible for preparing and approving the accounts.

Many of the items to be dealt with in a company's accounts can be treated in several ways, each of which will have a different impact on that year's profits. Research and development expenditure is a particularly relevant example of the kind of item for which there is no prescribed method of treatment in the accounts. Some companies will take the cautious view that all such expenditure should be written off in the period in which it is incurred, while others may decide that if the project shows reasonable prospects of being potentially capable of commercial exploitation, the cost should be carried forward to be charged against the profits of later years as and when they are deemed to have benefited thereby.

Similarly, if a company embarks on a costly advertising campaign towards the end of its financial year, the directors may decide that the cost should be carried forward as a charge against the following year's profits because it is considered that this is the period which will enjoy the greatest advantage from the expenditure.

The income which is brought into account in any one financial year will include not only those sales for which payment has been received during the period but also any sales of goods which had been delivered and invoiced but remained unpaid at the close of the year. The amount of these unpaid sales will, of course, be represented in the balance sheet among the debtors shown under the classification of Current Assets.

Similarly, the costs that are brought into charge in the year's accounts will be adjusted to allow for payments already made which relate to subsequent accounting periods and for expenses that have accrued but which do not yet appear in the books of account.

In the case of a manufacturing business, a major factor which governs the ascertainment of trading profits is the adjustment that has to be made for the difference between the opening and closing stocks of raw materials and work in progress.

Obviously the whole of the materials purchased for stock during the course of the year will not have been consumed in the production processes when the books are closed at the end of the financial year, and it is therefore necessary to prepare an inventory of the materials and semi-finished goods represented in work in progress valued at the lower of cost price or market value. This stock in hand will, of course, already have gone through the books as expenditure incurred, but because it is not chargeable against the current year's trading it must be shown as a deduction against the costs of that period and carried forward as an opening charge against the following year's trading revenue.

By making these adjustments for the opening and closing stocks it is possible to determine the cost of the materials consumed during the financial period, as the following example shows:

	£
Opening stocks	150,000
Purchases during year	1,275,000
	1,425,000
Less: Closing stocks	175,000
Cost of materials consumed	£1,250,000

A typical Profit and Loss Account for a manufacturing company is given on page 56. This method of presentation discloses a logical sequence of events, starting with the year's sales and adding or deducting the increase or decrease in the value of stock and work in progress during the period so as to give the total Value of Production. From this figure is deducted the materials, direct labour and factory overheads costs to give the Manufacturing Profit, and thereafter the Selling, Distribution and Administration costs to give the Net Profit before Tax.

This form of presentation is one that might be

Profit and Loss Account–year ending December 31st, 197–

	£	£
Sales		4,150,000
Increase/Decrease in Stock and Work in Progress		25,000
Value of Production		4,175,000
Materials Purchased	1,275,000	
Direct Labour	600,000	
Factory Overheads	1,295,000	
		3,170,000
Manufacturing Profit		1,005,000
Selling Expenses	250,000	
Distribution Expenses	340,000	
Administration Expenses	210,000	
		800,000
Trading Profit		205,000
Investment Income		25,000
Net Profit (before Tax)		230,000
Corporation Tax		80,000
Net Profit (after Tax)		150,000
Dividends:		
Preference – 7%	14,000	
Ordinary – 15%	90,000	
		104,000
Profit Retained in the Business		£46,000

adopted for management purposes and it therefore gives considerably more detail than would be required to comply with the accounting disclosure requirements of the Companies Act, 1967, or than would normally be made available to the shareholders in the annual report.

Although the Companies Act, 1967, requires that the annual turnover should be disclosed in the published accounts, other information relating to such matters as materials, direct labour and overheads costs is not within the scope of this legislation. However, such information would be essential to the detailed analysis of a company's operating efficiency and cost structure.

CHAPTER SEVEN

Interpreting the Accounts – I

Although the primary role of published company accounts is to provide the shareholders with a report on the directors' stewardship of their invested capital, nowadays they are required to serve a number of other equally important functions.

Bank managers rely on them as a source of information when assessing a business's potential security as a borrower, trade credit inquiry agencies use them to supplement reports from other sources on the firm's credit-worthiness, and stockbrokers and investment analysts are dependent on them as a source of primary data for evaluating the company's shares as a prospective investment for recommendation to their clients.

Each of these experts will look to different aspects of the company's accounts when making an assessment for the particular purpose he has in mind, although, despite the new requirements of the Companies Act, 1967, governing disclosure in published accounts, the relatively limited amount of information normally given is often insufficient for making a detailed appraisal without being supplemented from other sources.

However, the internal financial statements that are normally produced for management use do not suffer from this disadvantage and can be analysed in greater detail if so required.

When assessing his company's overall performance, the manager is bound to judge it in the first instance from the viewpoint of the shareholders whose invested funds are in his charge, and in this respect he must relate it to the results achieved by comparable companies in similar industries.

Profitability. The most effective yardstick by which the financial performance of individual companies can be assessed and related to that of others is by comparing their respective profit-earning capacities expressed as a rate of return on capital employed. This return on capital employed ratio, while not applicable to every type of company, provides a yardstick by which the many interacting factors that govern business performance can be reduced to a single common denominator.

The ratio is calculated by expressing net profit as a percentage of the total capital funds employed in the business. The total of these funds is represented by the sum of the fixed and current assets, less the current liabilities, and it is customary to relate them to the net profit before taxation, as the level of taxation is almost wholly determined by government policy and is only marginally influenced by managerial action.

Applying this ratio to our imaginary company, the rate of return on capital employed would be calculated as follows:

	£
Net Profit (before tax)	230,000
Capital Employed:	
Fixed assets	1,075,000
Net current assets	420,000

$$\frac{£230,000}{£1,495,000} \times \frac{100}{1} = 15\cdot4\%$$

This ratio applies the acid test of management efficiency and provides a focal point from which are derived the other financial ratios that are used to assess specific aspects of business performance (See also Chapter 10).

Ratios which are prepared and considered in isolation are of little practical value, for it is only by comparing them with those of previous periods or with those of other companies operating in similar industries that meaningful conclusions can be drawn. Thus, if the comparison is made with earlier accounting periods it is possible to judge if the trend of profitability is towards improvement or decline and the reasons for any variation can be subject to further analysis.

However, when comparing performance with that of other companies, care must be taken to ensure that the comparison is being made on the basis of financial information deriving from a common base.

Thus, the following example of two imaginary companies operating in the same industry, but with different approaches to the problem of financing their expenditure on capital equipment, illustrates the kind of pitfall that has to be avoided by the financial analyst.

Company A leases its buildings and much of its plant and machinery, thereby employing total capital resources of £400,000. It has an annual turnover of £900,000 on which it earns profits of £60,000, thus yielding a return of 15 per cent on capital employed.

Company B owns its buildings, plant and machinery and has a total capital employed of £600,000, and on a similar turnover of £900,000 it shows a profit of £72,000, giving a corresponding return of 12 per cent on capital.

It will be seen that despite the broad similarities between the two companies, the different methods by which they finance their capital expenditure results in a significant variation in the yields achieved on their respective capitals employed. It is therefore apparent that it would be unwise to conclude from a straight comparison of the rates of return being achieved on capital employed that the management of Company A is necessarily more efficient in its utilization of the capital resources which are available to it.

The lesson which might be learned from a comparison of the relative merits of owning or leasing fixed assets is that it may prove more profitable, in terms of the relative rates of return on capital, for a company to sell its freehold interests to a property company and lease them back on a long term basis. It is possible that such an evaluation will show that the funds thus released can be more profitably employed in other trading activities.

Equally misleading results might derive from a comparison of the performances of companies that are operating in dissimilar industries. The impact of government economic policy can vary considerably from industry to industry, particularly in regard to such factors as changes in the rates of purchase tax or hire purchase deposit and repayment regulations. Profit margins within individual industries will also be conditioned by the available production capacity and state of consumer demand. These factors, and many others, will combine to produce differing trading patterns that can vitiate useful comparisons of performance between companies which might otherwise bear a strong outward resemblance.

Because the rate of profit earned on capital employed may well be affected by factors of a predominantly financial nature, a useful check on the commercial success of management, as represented by the consistency with which profit margins on sales are maintained, is provided by the percentage ratio of net profit (before tax) to turnover (annual sales). In the case of our imaginary company, this ratio is calculated as follows:

$$\text{Trading profit} = \pounds 205,000$$
$$\text{Turnover} = \pounds 4,150,000$$
$$\frac{\pounds 205,000}{\pounds 4,150,000} \times \frac{100}{1} = 4 \cdot 94\%$$

If the company's management has applied a consistent 'mark up' policy when calculating selling prices, this ratio could be expected to remain fairly constant from one period to another and would hardly be affected by financial factors that bear mainly on the capital employed side of the equation; an example of this latter being a slackening of credit control procedures with a consequent increase in the amount of capital tied up in outstanding customer accounts.

However, the rate of profit earned on sales has an obvious bearing on the ultimate rate of profit earned on capital, depending on the ratio between capital employed and turnover. Thus, a company which earns $7\frac{1}{2}$ per cent on turnover and has a capital employed/turnover ratio of $1:2$ will show a return on capital of 15 per cent by the end of the financial year, having 'turned over' its capital twice during that period. On the other hand, another company which earns the same rate of profit on sales may have a capital employed/turnover ratio of $1:1\cdot5$ and will thus show a return on capital of $11\frac{1}{4}$ per cent.

It will be seen from these examples that the higher the

ratio between turnover and capital employed, the narrower will be the profit margin, expressed as a percentage of selling price, that will be required to produce a given rate of return on capital. Thus, a business such as a departmental store which purchases from its suppliers on credit terms, holds minimal trading stocks, and sells to its customers on strict cash terms, can afford to accept a very small margin of profit on each transaction.

Conversely, a company that operates in an industry that has a lengthy manufacturing cycle (eg ship-building), requiring a considerable investment in work-in-progress, has to earn a much higher relative rate of profit on each transaction so as to achieve a comparable rate of return on capital employed.

Liquidity. Profitability is only one aspect of business performance and although a firm may be achieving a good rate of earnings, it is still possible for it to encounter difficulties in meeting its day-to-day payment commitments because of excessive investment of working capital resources in stock, work in progress and trade debts.

The extent of its commitments in this respect can be assessed from an examination of the current assets and current liabilities items in the balance sheet, viz:

Current Assets	£
Stock and Work in Progress	540,000
Debtors	635,000
Treasury Bills	15,000
Tax Reserve Certificates	25,000
	1,215,000

Current Liabilities	
Creditors	508,000
Bank Overdraft	135,000
Taxation	48,000
Proposed Dividends	104,000
	795,000
Net Current Assets	£420,000

It will be seen that apart from a total of £152,000 which becomes payable in respect of dividends and taxation, there is a liability of £508,000 relating to outstanding creditors' accounts for materials and services supplied, and these commitments will, in the normal course of events, have to be discharged within one or two months of the balance sheet date. The sources to which the management must look to provide the funds from which payment can be made are to a large extent represented by the debtors item of £635,000.

This amount normally comprises the balances owed by customers in respect of goods invoiced on monthly account terms and it can therefore be expected that the greater part of these debts will have been paid within two or three months of the balance sheet date. In this event there will be a sufficient flow of cash to provide the funds needed to meet the creditors' accounts which become due for settlement within this period of time.

In the event of the debtors' balances being exceeded in total by the outstanding creditors' accounts, then any shortfall would have to be made good by an increase in the bank borrowings beyond the amount of the overdraft as it stands in the balance sheet. It is not possible, of course, to ascertain from a company's published accounts the full extent of its potential bank borrowing facility and it would be most unwise to assume that the actual amount of the overdraft (if any) shown in the balance sheet represents this limit. However, any business that shows a liability to creditors in excess of the balances payable by its debtors should certainly be regarded as being potentially deficient of adequate working capital.

If the trading stock figure includes a significant volume of finished goods that is likely to be converted into *cash* sales within a few weeks of the balance sheet date, this will, of course, represent a more favourable position than is immediately apparent from the accounts. However, the published value of stock is not normally analysed into its constituent elements of raw materials, work in progress and finished goods, and so this information would not be available except as the result of specific inquiry.

CURRENT ASSETS/CURRENT LIABILITIES RATIO

One of the tests of liquidity that is frequently advocated is the application of the current assets/current liabilities ratio to a company's balance sheet. In the case of the figures quoted above, the ratio is:

Current Assets	£1,215,000	
Current Liabilities	£795,000	
£1,215,000:£795,000	::	1·53:1·0

Any narrowing of this ratio may indicate a deterioration in the company's liquid position and should therefore be regarded as a warning signal, particularly if the trend continues over a series of financial periods.

However, this particular ratio is of limited value as a

means of comparing the relative liquid positions of two or more companies, as such factors as normal credit terms, stock financing arrangements, etc, may vary widely and thus vitiate comparisons.

The use of ratios as a method of controlling liquidity will be dealt with in greater detail in a subsequent chapter.

CAPITAL EXPENDITURE

When assessing a company's ability to meet the demands on its working capital resources, it is important to consider any outstanding commitments in respect of capital expenditure projects and contingent liabilities which have not been taken into consideration in preparing the accounts.

The Companies Act, 1967, requires companies to append a note to their published accounts giving a general indication of items of this nature, and it is therefore possible to relate these commitments to the available liquid or near-liquid resources shown under the heading of Current Assets.

Similarly, of course, if the company has an issue of loan stock which is approaching its redemption date, then a material factor in assessing its liquid position would be the adequacy of the resources or the nature of the arrangements made for providing the funds from which redemption will be effected.

To the extent that the company owns the freehold of its premises (if any) and they have not already been charged to secure earlier borrowings, they would constitute a potentially valuable backing to support a fund-raising operation.

CHAPTER EIGHT

Interpreting the Accounts — II

In the previous chapter we considered the interpretation of accounts from the external balance sheet aspect, being primarily concerned with yardsticks for assessing overall profitability and the business's ability to maintain its liquidity. We must now consider the kind of yardsticks and measurements to look for in assessing the business in relation to its trading activities as they would be seen from the viewpoint of the departmental manager.

Because of the diverse nature of business activities, from distribution and retailing to heavy manufacture, from merchant banking to airline operation, it is not possible to suggest a concise summary of the kind of information which should be looked for in the manufacturing or profit and loss account. In one industry close control of revenue may be the vital factor, while in another careful and accurate assessment of capital expenditure may be of greatest importance.

However, so far as it is possible to offer any generalizations in a field where each firm is likely to consider itself unique, these will be related to the affairs of an imaginary manufacturing business, based on the following trading accounts produced at monthly or four-weekly intervals. The business is assumed to have three distinct manufacturing activities which are independent of each other except to the extent that they share common works services, and selling, distribution and administrative facilities.

	A	B	C	Total
	£	£	£	£
Sales	45,000	82,000	29,000	156,000
Increase/Decrease in Stocks	5,000	(7,000)	1,000	(1,000)
Value of Production	50,000	75,000	30,000	155,000
Materials	20,000	27,000	10,000	57,000
Labour	7,000	6,000	4,000	17,000
Factory Overheads				
Fixed	3,000	16,000	2,000	21,000
Variable	5,000	6,000	4,000	15,000
	35,000	55,000	20,000	110,000
Manufacturing Profit	15,000	20,000	10,000	45,000

Selling Expenses	10,000	
Distribution Expenses	12,000	
Administration Expenses	8,000	
		30,000
Trading Profit		£15,000

With monthly trading profit statements produced in this form, showing a departmental analysis of costs and revenue, the management has the basis for much useful information on the profitability, both present and prospective, for each of the major activities.

A useful starting point for this assessment is to express these departmental figures in terms of relative percentages, viz:

	A	B	C
	%	%	%
Materials	40·0	36·0	33·3
Labour	14·0	8·0	13·3
Factory Overheads			
Fixed	6·0	21·3	6·7
Variable	10·0	8·0	13·4
Manufacturing Profit	30·0	26·7	33·3
Value of Production	100·0	100·0	100·0

Manufacturing Profit – A 33·3%
– B 44·4%
– C 22·3%

It will be seen that at this level of turnover 44·4 per cent of the Manufacturing Profit has been derived from Department B, although the rate of profit, expressed as a percentage of turnover, is the lowest of the three. However, assuming that the variable overheads element in each of the departmental analyses fluctuates in direct proportion to the sales (not necessarily a safe assumption in every case), each £100 of turnover will make a contribution of £26·7 towards the total manufacturing profit. The corresponding contributions from Departments A and C would be £30·0 and £33·3 respectively.

Because of the varying proportions of fixed overheads in the departmental cost structures, the effect of an increase in turnover on their profitability will vary considerably. For example, if we assume that each department is able to increase its turnover in volume and in value by 20 per cent, with comparable increases in materials, labour and variable overheads, their relative trading figures would be as follows:

	A		B		C	
	£	%	£	%	£	%
Value of Production	60,000	100·0	90,000	100·0	36,000	100.0
Materials	24,000	40·0	32,400	36·0	12,000	33·3
Labour	8,400	14·0	7,200	8·0	4,800	13·3
Factory Overheads						
Fixed	3,000	5·0	16,000	17·8	2,000	5·6
Variable	6,000	10·0	7,200	8·0	4,800	13·3
	41,400		62,800		23,600	
Manufacturing Profit	18,600	31·0	27,200	30·2	12,400	34·5

The respective percentage contributions made by each department towards the total Manufacturing Profit are A – 32·0; B – 46·7; C – 21·3, showing a marked relative increase in the profitability of department B. This arises from the gearing factor introduced into its cost structure by the higher proportion of fixed overheads (See also Chapter 12).

It is often the case that firms which are more labour intensive in their cost structures will have a higher proportion of direct labour, with a resulting tendency for their major expense items to be of a variable nature. Conversely, a capital intensive structure normally indicates a lesser dependence on the use of labour but with the consequent penalty of a higher level of fixed costs and therefore a higher break even point.

Wherever possible, sales and production figures should be expressed in terms of quantities as well as values, for by so doing it is possible to obtain a better indication of the extent to which variations in profitability are due to price changes or product mix rather than to changes in output rates.

An analysis of sales volume which reveals that the

half-year's revenue yield of £377,000 represented a
quantitative sale of 130,000 units of output at an average
price of £2·90, compared with the previous period's
sale of 120,000 units which yielded £360,000 at an
average price of £3, will offer a more useful basis for
subsequent decision-making than would a simple comparison of the revenue for the two periods.

ADDED VALUE

A useful measure of internal efficiency is provided by
the relationship of Direct Labour costs to the Added
Value for the period. The Added Value is represented
by the Value of Production less the cost of bought out
materials and components. As the descriptive title of
the term suggests, it is that part of the eventual sales
value that is contributed by the firm in the form of
labour and factory overhead expenditure. Using the
figures in the specimen trading account illustrated
earlier in this chapter (page 68), the respective departmental figures for Added Value would be calculated as
follows:

	Department A	Department B	Department C
	£	£	£
Value of Production	50,000	75,000	30,000
Less: *Materials*	20,000	27,000	10,000
Added Value	30,000	48,000	20,000

In practice it might be necessary to make an adjustment to these figures to take account of significant
variations (if any) in the materials content of the opening and closing stock valuations.

When these figures are related to the respective

labour costs of the three departments, the following
ratios of Added Value to Labour costs are derived:

	A £	B £	C £
Added Value	30,000	48,000	20,000
Labour	7,000	6,000	4,000
Added Value/ Labour Ratio	4·3	8·0	5·0

Although these figures do not reveal much when they
are viewed in isolation, they will, if compared with those
of earlier or subsequent periods, give an indication of the
increase or decrease in the efficient use of resources per
£1 of labour. Thus, assuming that in a later period
materials costs had increased by 10 per cent and labour
costs by 5 per cent, without any corresponding increase
in selling prices, a similar calculation would reveal the
following ratios:

	A £	B £	C £
Value of Production	50,000	75,000	30,000
Less: Materials	22,000	29,700	11,000
Added Value	28,000	45,300	19.000
Labour	7,350	6,300	4,200
Added Value/ Labour Ratio	3·8	7·2	4·5

It will be seen that in each instance the Added Value/
Labour ratio has shown a marked decrease, indicating
the greater amount of 'work' required from each £1 of
labour to produce the same Value of Production.

During times of trade recession and falling profit
margins the attentions of management are frequently

turned towards means of achieving economies in expenditure, and when such a course of action seems to be desirable a close examination of the accounts will often reveal those areas which are most likely to provide a source of such economies.

In the case of the imaginary firm whose accounts have formed the basis for the explanations in this chapter, it will, for example, be seen that 37 per cent of the Value of Production is represented by bought out materials and components. Thus, even a moderate cut of 1 per cent on the total of £57,000 spent in this way during the month would yield a cost reduction of £570, whereas a similar rate of reduction on the payroll of £17,000 would show a very much lower yield. With fixed overheads standing at £21,000, there is probably little to be gained in the short term from economies among the major items within this category. The principal categories of expenditure charged under this heading normally include such items as depreciation of buildings and plant (or the equivalent rent), rates, insurances, managerial and supervisory salaries, and other overheads which cannot yield an early reduction without seriously impairing the firm's ultimate power of recovery.

At times of financial stringency it is usually relatively easily-controlled expenditure, such as press advertising, which feels the first impact of the economy axe, although it is sometimes argued that at a time when sales are falling this is not the occasion for reducing expenditure aimed towards obtaining more business.

The assessment and interpretation of financial information relating to overhead expenditure cannot always be reduced to the statistical formulae that sometimes applies to direct labour and materials costs. It is therefore often necessary to rely on a well-founded system of budgetary control such as is outlined elsewhere in this volume.

LONG TERM TRENDS

It is natural that managements should tend to pay particular attention to the figure of monthly sales as being the principal yardstick of their success in running the business at a profit, but where the nature of the major activities results in a seasonal pattern of trade it is not always easy to detect from month to month if the trend of sales is up or down.

However, by preparing a Moving Annual Total of sales (see also Chapter Seventeen) it is possible to assess the trend of sales irrespective of short term seasonal fluctuations.

The following example illustrates the application of the MAT (Moving Annual Total) technique to the monthly turnover figures of an imaginary company.

	Monthly Sales		
	Year 1	*Year* 2	*MAT*
	£'000	£'000	£'000
January	100	90	1,345
February	90	85	1,340
March	100	95	1,335
April	105	95	1,325
May	110	100	1,315
June	130	120	1,305
July	145	125	1,285
August	150	135	1,270
September	130	120	1,260
October	120	115	1,255
November	90	95	1,260
December	85	90	1,265

The Moving Annual Total of sales in the third column represents an accumulated total for the immediately preceding twelve months (thus the total of £1,345,000 at January represents the total of the twelve months from February of Year 1 through to January of Year 2), thereby giving a progressive annual sales turnover figure which smooths out seasonal fluctuations and discloses the true trend. It will be seen from this particular example that the business experienced a declining rate of annual turnover throughout Year 2, until the month of November when there were signs of a slight recovery.

It will assist in appreciating the reasons for a change in the trend of sales if the money values of the sales figures are supported by corresponding physical quantities – eg tons, units, ton/miles, etc – particularly if this information is analysed on a departmental or other appropriate basis.

CHAPTER NINE

Capitalization and Gearing

The principal characteristics of the various types of share and loan capital were considered in an earlier chapter and it is now time to examine in detail their advantages and disadvantages in relation to the requirements of the company's overall capital structure.

Essentially, of course, all investors who put their capital into industrial and commercial companies knowingly accept a greater element of risk in the expectation that their investment will, over a period of time, earn a higher rate of return than they could expect from government stocks and similar securities.

However, even with industrial investment, the need often arises to grade the risks and the corresponding rates of return so as to meet the special requirements of particular situations. Every company must, of course, have a basic element of risk-bearing ordinary shareholders – the investors of last resort who accept the possibility of participating in any large rewards which might accrue from the company's prosperity in return for accepting the equally likely possibility that they might lose both their income and their capital.

The reasons that lead a company to adopt a particular form of capitalization will depend very much on the circumstances in which it finds itself at the time when it is seeking to raise new finance. It may be that because there is an extra element of risk involved, any new investors could only be attracted by offering preference shares with specially generous dividend rights attaching to them – or, conversely, because the company shows good prospects of future profits newcomers can be persuaded to put their money into the business in the form of ordinary shares, and are ready to forego immediate dividends in anticipation of greater rewards to come.

Not all these considerations can be expressed in terms of relative risks, however, for as the taxation law stands at the present time there are sound financial reasons for favouring loan capital rather than attempting to raise new funds by an issue of share capital.

Whereas distributions of income to shareholders in the form of dividends have to be made out of the residue of taxed profits, the interest which is paid to holders of loan stock is allowed as a charge against taxable profits before striking the balance on which the liability is assessed.

This difference in taxation treatment enhances the value of the 'gearing' factor which is introduced when a company raises a part of its capital requirements in the form of fixed interest loans.

The significance of capital gearing can best be illustrated by an example which compares the position of the Ordinary shareholders of a company that has a mixed capital structure of Preference and Ordinary shares and Loan Stock with the position as it would be if its capital was comprised wholly of Ordinary Shares.

The assumed capital structure of the company in both these cases is as follows:

	'Mixed' Capital £	Wholly Ordinary Capital £
Share Capital		
7% Preference Shares £1 ea.	200,000	—
Ordinary Shares £1 ea.	800,000	1,500,000
Reserves	370,000	370,000
6% Loan Stock	500,000	—
Total Funds	1,870,000	1,870,000

If the company were to earn trading profits of £400,000 (before tax) the relative position of the Ordinary shareholders would be markedly different in the two cases, viz:

	'Mixed' Capital £	Wholly Ordinary Capital £
Trading Profit before tax	400,000	400,000
Interest on 6% Loan Stock	30,000	—
	370,000	400,000
Corporation Tax at 40%	148,000	160,000
	222,000	240,000
Preference Dividend 7%	14,000	—
Balance available for Ordinary Shareholders	£208,000	£240,000
Ordinary Shareholders' Funds	£1,170,000	£1,870,000
Net Earnings on Ordinary Shareholders' Funds	17·8%	12·9%

It is apparent that in the case where the company is financed wholly by Ordinary share capital, the absence of prior charges on income in the form of Preference

dividends and Loan Stock interest entitles the Ordinary
shareholders to the whole of the after-tax surplus. However, because they have contributed the whole of the
permanent share capital, the rate of earnings on their
funds has decreased from 17·8 to 12·9 per cent.

The advantages to be gained by the introduction of
prior charge capital offer a considerable inducement in
favour of this form of capitalization, but there are corresponding disadvantages which must be borne in mind,
particularly if there is a tendency for trading profits to
fluctuate from year to year.

The Preference dividend and Loan Stock interest
constitute a fixed annual commitment which, at least
in the case of the latter, must be paid regardless of the
sufficiency of profits from which to meet them. Thus, in
years when trading profits have shown a fall these prior
charges on earnings can become a source of embarrassment, as can be demonstrated by showing the position
of the company in the previous example when its
trading profits have fallen to £160,000.

	'Mixed' Capital £	Wholly Ordinary Capital £
Trading Profit before tax	160,000	160,000
Interest on 6% Loan Stock	30,000	—
	130,000	160,000
Corporation Tax at 40%	52,000	64,000
	78,000	96,000
Preference Dividend 7%	14,000	—
Balance available for Ordinary Shareholders	£64,000	£96,000
Net earnings on Ordinary Shareholders' Funds	5·5%	5·1%

In this example it will be seen that the earnings differential has virtually disappeared and with a further fall in trading profits the advantage conferred on the Ordinary Shareholders by this gearing factor would in fact become a liability.

PREFERENCE SHARES AND LOAN STOCK

The case for raising new capital in the form of Preference Shares has been considerably weakened by the changes in treatment of taxation on dividends introduced by the Finance Act, 1965. Before the passing of that legislation the company was permitted to retain the tax deducted from dividend payments and treat it as a part-recovery of the income tax already borne on trading profits, but under the new Corporation Tax regime such deductions from dividends must be accounted for separately and paid over to the Inland Revenue.

When this new method of treatment is compared with the more favourable treatment of Loan Stock and similar fixed loan interest referred to earlier in this chapter, it will be seen that the advantage has swung decisively in favour of this latter form of capitalization. Moreover, the fact that preference share capital is not redeemable (although issues of redeemable preference shares are permitted by the Companies Act, 1948 under certain conditions), whereas loan stock is more often than not issued subject to specific terms for redemption, does give the latter a greater degree of flexibility. Thus, if a company is forced to raise additional capital at a time when the general level of interest rates is high, then by fixing a date (or dates) for future redemption it becomes possible for it to re-fund its requirements at a more favourable rate of interest when the opportunity offers.

BANK LOANS AND OVERDRAFTS

Companies that enjoy the confidence of their bankers and are able to obtain good credit facilities to meet their daily working capital requirements are thereby able to gain all the benefits of this gearing factor. So long as they are able to earn a rate of return on these borrowed funds which is greater than the rate which they are required to pay their bankers for the use of this facility, there is every incentive to make the greatest possible use of their bank overdraft. Furthermore, the overdraft interest is an admissible charge for tax purposes and there is thus an added reason for using bank credit whenever possible.

SUPPLIERS' CREDIT

Although the benefit of short term credit granted by suppliers is to a large extent offset by the corresponding credit which has to be extended to customers, nevertheless any special credit facilities which can be obtained without resulting in noticeably higher prices will make a marginal contribution to an enhanced overall rate of return on the capital funds employed.

CHAPTER TEN

Accountancy as a Management Tool

Although accountancy is still to a very large extent concerned with its reporting and stewardship functions, increasingly greater emphasis is being placed on its more active role of providing a comprehensive financial service to assist managers in formulating trading policies and administering the departments and functions for which they are responsible.

This transition from a passive to an active role in business management has evolved over a number of years, but one of the greatest single factors which served to influence trends of thought within the accountancy profession was the report prepared by the (then) Anglo-American Productivity Council's Management Accountancy team which visited the United States of America in 1950 to examine the techniques which were being used with notable success in that country and to make recommendations as to how they might be applied in United Kingdom industry.

The team's report made a considerable impact on accounting thinking and provided a catalyst for the movement among accountants and managers towards the provision of more meaningful financial information than had hitherto been available in the majority of British companies.

THE PROFIT TARGET

Because all business activity is eventually measured in monetary terms, the acid test of managerial efficiency must be the rate of profit earned on the capital funds which have been entrusted to its stewardship. This is the standard by which it will eventually be judged and it therefore follows that the objective of all managerial planning must be aimed towards its maximization.

The profit rate which might reasonably be expected from the individual firm will, of course, depend on such factors as the average rate being achieved by other firms operating in the same or similar lines of business, the economic environment in which it finds itself trading at the time, and such other considerations as whether by the nature of its business it is capital intensive and requires the investment of substantial funds in buildings, plant, and other physical assets.

The fixing of the target rate of return on capital will usually be a matter for decision by the company's board of directors and in setting this objective they will be guided by these general considerations.

For the purpose of profit planning the management of the business will need to relate this target rate of return to the capital funds which come within their sphere of responsibility. In the case of our imaginary company whose balance sheet is shown on page 51, the amount of capital employed in the business is represented by the total of the fixed and current assets, less the current liabilities, viz:

	£
Fixed Assets	775,000
Investments	190,000
Current Assets	1,215,000
	2,180,000
Less: Current Liabilities	795,000
Capital Employed	£1,385,000

This figure of capital employed – £1,385,000 – therefore represents the invested capital which is expected to yield the required rate of return in the form of trading profit. Thus, if the company's board of directors had decided that the required rate of return was to be 15 per cent on capital employed, then the management would have to plan for a trading profit of approximately £210,000

$$\left(\text{viz. } \frac{15}{100} \times £1,385,000 = £210,000\right).$$

However, it is important to bear in mind that the figure at which such assets as freehold premises are included in this statement of capital employed does not necessarily represent their current market valuation, and if a more realistic target were to be set the capital employed base should be adjusted to bring them to a more appropriate figure. Thus, if the present value of the buildings was estimated to be £500,000 (as against the written down figure of £345,000), then the total figure of capital employed should be increased by £155,000 and this would result in a revised profit figure of £230,000.

It should also be noted that the figure of total capital

employed includes £190,000 representing funds utilized
in the acquisition of interests in subsidiary and associated
companies, and from the viewpoint of the managers
who are concerned with the profit-earning capacity of
the principal company, their profit target would be adjusted to exclude the funds so employed. In this event
the revised profit target would be calculated thus:

	£
Fixed Assets	775,000
Adjustment to bring freehold premises to current valuation	155,000
	930,000
Current Assets	1,215,000
	2,145,000
Less: Current Liabilities	795,000
	£1,350,000
Profit Target 15 per cent thereon =	£202,500

The profit targets for the managements of the individual subsidiary companies would be the subject of a
separate calculation related to the amount of capital
employed according to their own balance sheets.

It will be noted that the capital employed base
specifically excludes the sum of £110,000 shown in the
company's balance sheet as representing expenditure
incurred on acquiring goodwill, patents and trade marks
and this practice of ignoring intangible assets for the
purpose of calculating the return on capital employed
is usually followed by professional investment analysts.

However, depending on the nature of the intangible

assets and the circumstances in which they came to be acquired, it might be more relevant to the setting of the profit target to include an appropriate return for the funds which are employed in this way. For example, if the trade mark rights were acquired for the purpose of exploiting a particular product line, then it would seem logical to expect that the funds so utilized should yield their own contribution to profits (See also Chapter 7).

Too much target / budget associated.

THE TRADING BUDGET

Having defined its overall profit target, the firm's management must now set out to translate it into terms of a broad outline plan which will provide the blueprint for the forthcoming year's trading objectives.

Although this annual appraisal of business objectives is ultimately expressed in financial terms, it should not be regarded as an exercise which can be tackled by the company's financial director or accountant working in isolation. Indeed, the annual budget should be made the occasion for a searching scrutiny of all aspects of its expenditure, which in turn must entail consideration of policy at all levels of management.

Because it requires consideration of the whole spectrum of management activity, the most satisfactory way of achieving a co-ordinated plan is for the senior executives to constitute themselves as a budget committee which acts for the purpose of defining broad departmental objectives and scrutinizing expenditure proposals.

This concept of a group approach to business budgeting is essential to the preparation of a realistic and feasible trading plan, for without the co-operation and sense of commitment which flows from mutual agreement, albeit preceded by argument and discussion, there is every prospect that it will be discredited as something imposed from above without regard for trading circumstances. It therefore follows that if executives and departmental managers are brought into discussions and involved in the resulting decisions, they will implicitly accept a personal commitment to meet their objectives and the validity of the plan will be thus enhanced by its broad foundation of common acceptance.

One of the most useful by-products of this annual budgeting operation is the opportunity it offers for a critical appraisal of departmental functions and expenditures. All too often the daily pressures of routine give few occasions for the hard scrutiny that should be directed at all aspects of the organization and for this reason alone there is much to be said in favour of wide involvement at every level of managerial and supervisory responsibility.

Similarly, of course, by promoting the principle of delegating responsibility for control of spending, there is induced within the management structure a greater regard for the way in which funds are spent. If each departmental manager is made aware of his limits of spending power – limits which he has helped to fix himself – then he will be more conscious of the need to ensure that he gets value for money.

The starting point for the budget plan may either be the annual sales target or the annual production target, depending on the situation in which the business finds itself at that particular time. It is the exception rather than the rule for a firm to find itself in the situation where the demand for its products is evenly balanced by its capacity to produce the required output, and so its approach to the task of preparing the annual budget will be conditioned according to whether supply or demand is the limiting factor.

If present production capacity is more than adequate to meet orders in hand, then clearly the sales target is the limiting factor and must become the starting point for the budgeting operation – as would be the reverse case if there was an accumulated backlog of orders because of insufficient capacity to meet them.

The fixing of the sales target and the related output levels will rest with the sales manager and the production manager respectively and it is at this point that careful consideration will need to be given to any proposed product changes, price increases or other factors which are likely to be of material significance in this respect. It may be, of course, that when the budget has been completed it will be found that there is an insufficient profit margin to meet the requirements of the expected yield on capital employed, and in this eventuality further consideration may have to be given to the possibility of improving the sales target or effecting any necessary economies on spending proposals.

Concurrently with the preparation of the sales budget, similar estimates must be prepared of the production resources in terms of plant utilization, direct labour operatives and materials purchases required to fulfil this programme.

Factory overhead expenses, suitably allocated to budget cost centres under the control of the appropriate manager or supervisor, will similarly be estimated according to the scale of foreseen activity.

Spending allocations must also be agreed for the sales manager, categorized under appropriate budget headings (representatives' salaries and expenses, advertising, etc), and for the distribution and administrative activities of the business. Quite clearly, the cost of some of these functions will not fluctuate in proportion to the general level of trade activity, and in certain instances it can be argued that when business is slack then a strong case can be made out for increasing the rate of spending on advertising and related selling expenses. However, these are matters for decision at board level and if such a policy appeared to be justified, then the budget committee would submit its recommendation accordingly.

When preparing departmental budgets it is important to distinguish between those items of expense over which the individual manager can be expected to exercise some degree of control and expenses which arise from the past decisions of senior management or the board of directors.

The individual departmental manager can obviously influence spending on such items as wages (including overtime), electricity consumed by lighting and machinery within his department, materials, and other expenditure of a similar nature, and it is reasonable that these should be included within his specific budgetary allocation.

However, when considering such items as rent, rates, depreciation, the cost of service functions such as personnel services or the accounts department, it would be unreasonable to treat these as a direct charge to the individual manager's budget. When a budget is prepared in this way as a method of exercising financial expenditure control, as distinct from one which has been prepared for broad planning purposes, it must include only those items which it is within the manager's ability to influence in the short term.

The longer term types of expenditure are invariably

the result of past policy decisions and can often only be varied, if at all, as a result of fundamental changes. However, from the viewpoint of setting profit targets for individual departments, it is advisable to fix these at such a figure that proper allowance has been made for the recovery of that proportion of the fixed overheads expenditure which is regarded as being a fair burden to be met from its overall margin.

EXAMPLE

The Machining Department manager has been allocated a direct expenditure budget made up as follows:

DEPARTMENTAL BUDGET		£
Budgeted output (at selling price)		50,000
(representing 100,000 units at 50p per unit)		
Direct Expenditure	£	
Production materials	15,000	
Direct labour	10,000	
Supervisory wages	2,000	
Manager's salary	1,500	
Packing materials	500	
Other direct expenses	1,000	
		30,000
Departmental gross profit		20,000
Indirect Overheads contribution		10,000
Budgeted departmental net profit		£10,000

In this example the manager would be expected to exercise direct control over those items included under the heading of 'Direct Expenditure' and to make a sufficient margin of Departmental Gross Profit to ensure his contribution to the Indirect Overheads of the business.

However, by far the most important aspect of financial forecasting of the course of future trading is the wider plan covering the full range of activities.

The following simplified budget, based on the results portrayed in the Profit and Loss Account in Chapter 6, shows how such a financial plan might be evolved.

Downtown Electrics Ltd, manufactures and markets four basic products; an electric time switch, an electric egg whisk, a small electric motor, and a cheap electric razor. Three months before the beginning of its new financial year, which runs from January to December, the company's management starts to prepare the trading plan and budget.

The Sales Manager estimates that the company can hold its share of the potential market and will achieve the following sales level:

		£
800,000 electric time switches @ £1·50 ea.		1,200,000
200,000 electric egg whisks @ £2·50 ea.		500,000
850,000 electric motors @ £2·00 ea.		1,700,000
250,000 electric razors @ £3·00 ea.		750,000
		4,150,000

This turnover is within the existing productive capacity of the plant and the following estimates are made of the Materials and Labour elements.

Materials

The cost of materials is estimated as follows:

			£
800,000 switches	@	25p	200,000
200,000 whisks	@	72½p	145,000
850,000 motors	@	80p	680,000
250,000 razors	@	100p	250,000
			1,275,000

Labour

The direct labour force required to sustain this rate of output is estimated to be:

	£
1,000 female operatives @ £2 per day =	2,000
100 male operatives @ £5 per day =	500
Direct labour cost per working day	2,500

With 240 working days per annum, the estimated annual pay roll will be £600,000

It should be noted that Direct Labour costs exclude payments made to productive employees in respect of holiday pay. This expenditure is normally charged as a Factory Overheads item (see below).

Detailed budgets would be prepared for all the overheads expense items charged under the following headings:

Factory Overheads	£
Indirect Labour	350,000
Management and Supervision	80,000
Rates	25,000
Power, Lighting and Heating	50,000
Depreciation of Plant and Buildings	55,000
Indirect Materials and Expenses	150,000
Other Expenses	585,000
	1,295,000

Selling	
Promotion and Publicity	100,000
Representatives' Salaries and Expenses	100,000
Sales Office Expenses	30,000
Overseas Representation	20,000
	250,000

Distribution
Packing Charges
   Home   10,000
   Overseas   50,000
Motor Vehicle Fleet Expenses   180,000
Regional Warehouses   100,000

                                         340,000

Administration
Accounts Department   50,000
Establishment Expenses   80,000
Postage, Telephones, etc   10,000
Executive and other Administration Expenses   70,000

                                       210,000

If the above budget were to be fulfilled in every respect, the outcome of the year's trading would be as shown by the Profit and Loss Account in Chapter 6.

It is by preparing such a detailed study of every facet of the company's activities that the management can obtain a reliable forecast of the probable outcome of the coming year's trading.

It must be emphasized, of course, that such a budget plan is no more reliable than the sum total of the opinions that are represented in these estimates. However, it remains an essential prerequisite to any planning decisions and provides a blueprint from which can be charted the future course of trading.

CHAPTER ELEVEN

Financial Reporting

Just as the budget plan is built up by a careful assessment of manning requirements and estimated levels of spending in respect of each category of expenditure, so must the accounting system be devised to analyse and allocate these charges according to the budget centre under which they were authorized.

The larger the organization, the more difficult becomes the routine task of ensuring that items of expenditure are charged to the appropriate budget cost centre. The most satisfactory and easily applied method of ensuring this result, is to introduce a system of account code numbers which facilitates easy identification of expenditure.

The compilation of such a system of account codes, which can in some respects resemble the decimal classification adopted for library books, entails a close study of the types of expenditure incurred and their relationship to the company's administrative structure. Although the extent of the coding must obviously be kept within limits, so as not to unduly add to the number of account headings which must be maintained, the more explicit the definition of the type of expense to be charged against each number, the easier is the task of delegating individual spending responsibility.

As an elementary example of this precept, travelling expenses are incurred by a number of individuals within many companies and this type of expenditure can be analysed to a widely varying degree of detail. It can at one extreme be collated under one general code heading to cover all travelling expenses, and at the other it can be allocated as necessary to a separate code number to represent each individual department's spending under this classification.

The following is a simple system of account coding related to the expenditure headings used in the specimen budget in the previous chapter, although in practice the range of codes would be considerably extended beyond this brief selection of items.

Materials	100 – Steel strip
	101 – Steel plate
	102 – Moulding powder
Bought out components	200 – Fuses
	201 – Motors
	202 – Terminals
Labour – Direct	300 – Productive
	301 – Waiting time
	302 – Training time
Factory Overheads	400 – Indirect Labour
	401 – Management and Supervision
	402 – Rates
	403 – Power, Lighting and Heating
	404 – Depreciation – Plant and Buildings
	405 – Indirect Materials and Expenses
	406 – Other Expenses
Selling	500 – Promotion and Publicity
	501 – Representatives' Salaries and Expenses
	502 – Sales Office Expenses
	503 – Overseas Representation
Distribution	600 – Packing Charges – Home
	601 – Packing Charges – Overseas
	602 – Motor Vehicle Fleet Expenses
	603 – Regional Warehouses
Administration	700 – Accounts Department
	701 – Establishment Expenses
	702 – Postage, Telephones, etc
	703 – Executive and other Administration Expenses

AUTHORIZATION AND ALLOCATION OF
EXPENDITURE

The implementation of this coding system should begin with the purchasing procedure. The account code number against which the expenditure will eventually be charged will be allocated at the time when the buying order is initiated, thereby ensuring that when the supplier's invoice is received it can immediately be identified to the appropriate cost centre.

By adopting such a procedure, spending responsibility is ascertained before a liability has been incurred and the possibility of subsequent dispute is thus minimized. Furthermore, the accounting processes entailed in verifying and collating departmental costs are considerably eased, thus hastening the preparation of the expenditure statements which provide an essential part of the budgetary control system.

It is a necessary corollary of a successful system of budgetary control that not only does the individual department head who has been charged with the responsibility for controlling expenditure within a cost centre have a say in the preparation of the budget, but he must also be assured that the spending and allocation of expenditure against that budget should be within the scope of his authority.

To facilitate authorization of expenditure by the departmental head whose budget will eventually be charged, it is desirable that he, or his nominated representative, should approve and initial a copy of the purchase order before it is sent to the suppliers. When the invoice is eventually received it can be readily identified by reference to this copy order and thus allocated to its correct cost centre.

MEASURING BUDGET PERFORMANCE

Having defined its financial targets, represented by the annual trading budget, the company's management depends on the accounting system to provide regular reports that will measure subsequent performance against this yardstick.

This reporting procedure achieves its maximum effectiveness when it is applied on a departmental basis that corresponds with the cost centres that have provided the basic structure for the budget, and its application will be illustrated by reference to the departmental budget given in the previous chapter.

By fixing the budget targets in terms of labour manning requirements and levels of operating activity, the management has, by definition, set itself certain working standards to which it must seek to conform. For the purpose of checking its performance with these standards, the comparison can be most easily facilitated by relating the principal heads of expenditure (ie labour and overheads) to a basic standard unit of measurement – the value of a standard hour of work.

Thus, in the specimen departmental budget in the previous chapter, if we assume that the budgeted direct labour of £10,000 represented the cost of 10 male operatives working a 40-hour week for 240 days a year, the department's hourly labour rate would be calculated as follows:

$$\text{10 operatives} \times \text{8 hours} \times \text{240 days} = \text{19,200 hours}$$
$$\text{Annual labour budget} = £10,000$$
$$\therefore \text{Budgeted hourly labour rate} = \frac{£10,000}{19,200} = \text{52p per hour}$$

In the same way, a similar hourly rate can be

calculated for the budgeted overheads of the department, viz.

Overhead Expenses	£
Supervisory Wages	2,000
Manager's Salary	1,500
Packing Materials	500
Other Direct Expenses	1,000
Indirect Overheads	10,000
	15,000

$$\therefore \text{ Budgeted hourly rate} = \frac{£15,000}{19,200} = 78\text{p per hour}$$

Assuming that the actual labour and overheads costs for the period are £10,200 and £15,370 respectively and that the total of standard hours recovered is 19,100, the resulting performance could be expressed as follows:

LABOUR

Hours		Gain/Loss at 52p per hour		Expenditure variance	Net gain/loss
Budgeted	Recovered	Hours	£	£	£
19,200	19,100	100	52	200	252

OVERHEADS

Hours		Gain/Loss at 78p per hour		Expenditure variance	Net gain/loss
Budgeted	Recovered	Hours	£	£	£
19,200	19,100	100	78	370	448

By analysing the department's expenditure in terms of variances, it is possible to ascertain more precisely those factors, ie efficiency and over-spending, which contributed to the loss of profit.

The advantage of this method is that it illustrates very clearly by means of the efficiency variance, the extent to which profit margins are influenced by the degree of success or failure in achieving the budgeted volume of output.

This principle of measuring performance in relation to predetermined cost standards can be applied in very much greater detail to individual product lines which are operating within a department and the detailed techniques are dealt with in a later chapter.

CHAPTER TWELVE

Cost Behaviour

One of the most important aspects of a business's financial structure is the behaviour of the underlying costs. These costs can usually be identified as belonging to one of three categories (a) fixed costs, (b) variable costs, and (c) semi-variable costs.

Fixed costs are those expenditures which, broadly speaking, will continue to be incurred whatever the level of activity within the business. Rent and rates are typical examples of this category, being expenditures which cannot be avoided or reduced for so long as it is necessary for the business to maintain its capacity to produce. The extent to which expenditure is classified as a fixed cost depends to some extent on the time scale involved. In the short term a wide range of expenditures may come within the classification of fixed costs, but in the longer term many of them can be recategorized or entirely eliminated.

Thus, if the business employs a number of highly-skilled operatives who, because of the expense of re-training, would be difficult to replace if they were to leave, then in the event of it facing a recession it would probably be prepared to treat this part of the payroll as a short-term fixed cost. However, if the recession were to be prolonged and full employment could not be maintained, then undoubtedly some reduction in staffing would have to be faced.

At the other extreme, a manufacturing business whose

products embody an element of materials costs will undoubtedly find that this type of expenditure is truly variable and will rise or fall in direct proportion to any increase or decrease in the volume of output.

Expressed as a percentage of the value of a unit of output, the materials cost will maintain a constant relationship and total expenditure will rise in the same ratio as the volume of output.

Between these two extremes there is a wide range of costs that do not fall naturally into either of these categories. Such expense items as the telephone account have both a fixed element (the equipment rental charge) and a variable element (the cost of the calls made). Other types of expense remain constant within a certain range of activity but show a marked increase once operational requirements entail further expansion. Typical of this category of expenditure might be supervisory salaries, as the number of supervisory staff will normally remain constant despite fluctuations in the size of the payroll of productive employees, but may need to be increased if there is a major expansion in the scale of activities.

On a larger scale, the production capacity available from a factory might be capable of meeting all the foreseeable demand for its output, in which case such expense items as rent, rates and depreciation of plant and premises will not normally show any increase or decrease as a result of fluctuations in the level of production. On the other hand, if the available capacity is already fully utilized and the opportunity arises for the company to obtain further orders, then it is probable that the additional output which will be required can be obtained only from a further expansion of the existing facilities. Such an expansion of production capacity might be obtained from increased shift working using the existing plant, or, if this is not feasible, then by the installation of additional plant and machinery. It is possible that this expansion of facilities might even entail the acquisition of extra premises in which to accommodate the new equipment and additional operatives.

In this event, once the decision has been made to increase the base load facilities, there will be a major addition to the fixed expense burden in the form of rent, rates, depreciation, etc, on the newly-acquired premises and plant. Thus, the overall fixed expenses of the business will show an immediate increase at this point and create a major new factor in relation to production, marketing and pricing policies.

Illustrated in diagrammatic form, the pattern of these costs would appear as follows:

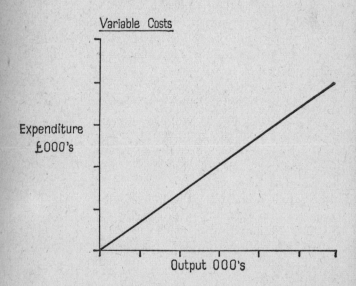

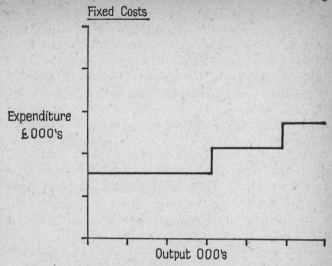

Thus, variable costs such as materials, labour, power, packing materials, etc, will show an increase in direct relationship to the level of production and their effect on unit costs will not normally alter at any point along the output scale – except to the extent that, for example, higher quantities may result in appropriate reductions in the purchase price of bought out parts and raw materials.

On the other hand, fixed costs will be incurred from the moment that the production facilities are created, even though production may not yet have commenced, and they will continue at this level, subject to relatively minor fluctuations, until the point is reached when another stage of expansion has to be embarked upon. When this happens, the fixed cost burden rises to its new level and will again continue until yet a further point of major expansion is reached.

It will be appreciated, of course, that having brought

additional production facilities into existence to meet the expanded demand for output, these extra costs are to a large extent permanently embedded in the fixed cost burden which the business has to bear, and any subsequent fall in output will not automatically produce a reduction in the fixed costs. Such reduction could only be brought about by disposing of some of the plant and that part of the premises which had previously been acquired to meet the demands of expansion.

BREAK EVEN POINT

By plotting these two cost curves on a single chart, it becomes easier to appreciate the effect of volume on the profitability of the business, viz:

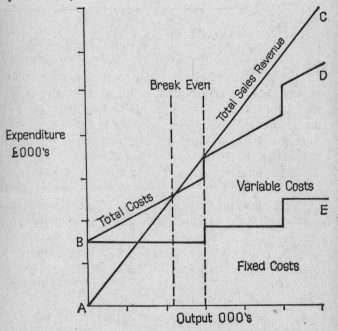

Assuming that the unit selling price of the company's products remains constant at any level of sales, the sales curve can be represented by the straight line AC. The fixed costs are represented by the line BE and the total costs (ie fixed and variable costs) by the line BD. Thus, as sales increase, the revenue curve rises to meet the total costs curve and at an output level of 2,200 units, the total revenue from sales is equal to total costs and the 'break even' point has been reached.

Further progression beyond this point will produce a trading profit, but it should be noted that the margin is narrowed when sales reach 3,000 units as a result of the extra band of fixed costs which it is necessary to incur at this point as additional facilities are provided to increase capacity to match the further projected increase in sales demand.

The point at which the break even position is reached will depend to a large extent on the type of cost structure. In the case of a business that requires a high investment of fixed capital in the form of complex and expensive machinery, with a consequent high depreciation charge, then the fixed cost element will be of greater significance and will defer the break even position to a point further up the cost scale. The following contrasting examples will help to illustrate the effect of different types of cost structures on the attainment of the break even position.

Company A has a high element of fixed costs, with consequent reduced variable costs, and achieves its break even position at about 40 per cent of capacity. Company B, with a much lower proportion of fixed costs but a larger element of variable costs, achieves its break even position at about 26 per cent of capacity.

A company that depends on labour rather than

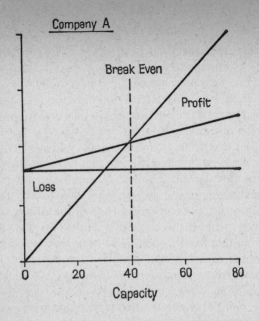

Company A

Break Even

Profit

Loss

| 0 | 20 | 40 | 60 | 80 |

Capacity

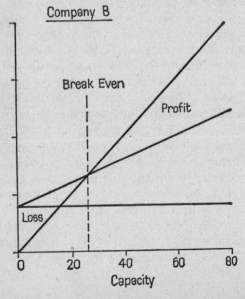

Company B

Break Even

Profit

Loss

| 0 | 20 | 40 | 60 | 80 |

Capacity

automatic machinery to achieve its output will tend to have higher variable costs with a consequent lower element of fixed costs, but should it decide to pursue a policy of automating its plant with the intention of reducing its dependence on the human element, then it has to accept the corollary that its higher break even point will necessitate a higher degree of plant utilization to maintain a reasonable rate of return on capital employed. It usually follows that the more flexible structure of the labour-intensive firm enables it to trim its costs (by, for example, reducing over-time or introducing short-time working) more rapidly than is possible for the capital-intensive firm with a high element of depreciation in its cost structure.

Conversely, under conditions of rapidly expanding demand for output, the company with a lower proportion of variable costs will often be at an advantage over companies that have a larger labour element in their costs. Because its additional output will yield a higher contribution to recovery of fixed costs, the greater degree of plant utilization achieved the greater will be the relative rate of return on capital employed.

The concept of the 'contribution factor' is in essence another aspect of the fixed costs/variable costs equation and its significance can best be explained by a simple example:

Company A and Company B market an identical product but because of differences in manufacturing methods their respective cost structures are as follows:

	Company A	Company B
	p	p
Materials	25	25
Labour	2½	12½
Overheads:		
Fixed	25	7½
Variable	10	17½
	62½	62½
Profit	7½	7½
Selling Price	70	70

It will be seen from these cost analyses that the variable cost elements of these two products are 37½p and 55p respectively, leaving in the case of Company A a contribution of 32½p towards fixed overheads and profit and in the case of Company B a contribution of 15p, viz:

	Company A	Company B
	p	p
Selling price	70	70
Less:		
Materials	25	25
Labour	2½	12½
Variable overheads	10	17½
Total variable costs	37½	55
Contribution to fixed overheads and profit	32½	15

It is readily apparent that Company A, with a contribution of 32½p per unit of output, obtains a larger gross profit margin when its cost structure is compared with Company B.

However, one of the most difficult aspects of preparing a calculation of this nature is to decide which costs are of a truly variable nature. In the circumstances mentioned above, during times of labour scarcity many firms would regard a significant proportion of their direct labour payroll as being in the nature of fixed costs, at least in the shorter term, and in consequence their actual break even point is higher than might be apparent from an analysis of costs prepared according to the conventional method by which direct labour costs are treated as a variable expense.

The contribution factor may be of particular significance when a decision has to be made on which of a range of products should be put into production – assuming, of course, that the available facilities are insufficient to manufacture them all and that the choice is to be made solely on the basis of profitability without regard to other possible commercial considerations.

As an example, we can consider the position of three alternative products whose selling prices and cost structures are as follows:

		Product A	Product B	Product C
		p	p	p
(a)	Selling price	120	100	95
	Materials	25	20	$22\frac{1}{2}$
	Labour	15	10	10
	Variable overheads	10	10	$7\frac{1}{2}$
(b)	Total variable costs	50	40	40
(c)	Contribution to fixed overheads and profit (a–b)	70	60	55
Hourly production rate (units)		290	370	380

At a first glance it might seem that Product A with the highest selling price and the largest contribution margin per unit might be the first choice for production. However, further examination would show that the highest hourly contribution rate is yielded by Product B, as will be apparent from the following figures:

	Product A	Product B	Product C
Total sales value per hour	£348	£370	£361
Total contribution per hour	£203	£222	£209

It may be, of course, that an adjustment of the selling price of Products A or C would alter the balance of advantage, but a knowledge of the prospective contribution rates is an essential prerequisite to a well-founded managerial decision.

It will be seen from this necessarily brief survey of cost behaviour that costing information may not always be what it seems to appear and without a clear understanding of the underlying financial elements it is possible to make a wrong decision because of a misinterpretation of the facts.

CHAPTER THIRTEEN

The Elements of Costing

Although industrial cost accounting is sometimes thought to be a difficult subject to understand, it is essentially a problem of clear thinking about fundamental principles and an eye for detail. Indeed, when it is reduced to its basic elements there is no reason why difficulty should be experienced in understanding what costing is all about.

Before starting to consider these principles and the related costing techniques, we might usefully remind ourselves of the purposes for which costing information is normally required. We can leave aside the special requirements of those costing systems which are maintained for such specialized purposes as fixing prices for application to Government contracts for stores purchases and research and development work.

Normally, costing information is required for three basic purposes: to provide the data from which price structures can be prepared as the basis for submitting quotations; to provide information on actual costs as a basis for comparison with the 'target' costs which are compiled for pricing purposes; to provide the information required for the purpose of valuing work in progress and finished goods for incorporation in inventory valuations in the annual and other periodic accounts.

In the case of costings prepared for quotation purposes it is often necessary to compile such information on the basis of estimates of output performance and materials and labour usage, particularly when the articles which are being costed have not previously been manufactured.

The principal elements of cost in a manufacturing business comprise the direct materials and components that are embodied in the product, the direct labour costs incurred in the actual processes of manufacture, and the wide range of indirect expenses which are incurred as a result of carrying on the overall manufacturing activities and which are normally aggregated under the collective description of 'Factory overheads'. To these items there must, of course, be added the further expenditures under the general headings of selling, distribution and administration.

It is important when preparing cost estimates for quotation purposes to take into consideration special expenditure such as tooling costs, setting charges and research and development expenditure. Such costs are usually recovered by making a special charge or alternatively by spreading the expenditure over the initial order or orders as an element of the individual unit cost.

Most costing problems resolve themselves into a question of allocation of expenditures and the more remote the individual item of expense becomes from the actual production process, the greater becomes the task of identifying it to a specific cost centre* and thus to the eventual cost of the individual product. Indeed, the major part of the expenditure incurred under the heading of factory overheads cannot generally be identified with specific departments or product lines.

On the other hand, purchases of raw materials and made out components can invariably be related to

* The term 'cost centre' is frequently met with in budgetary control and costing systems and it denotes a centre of activity to which items of identifiable cost can conveniently be allocated. It may be a workshop, a department, a production line or even a particular machine.

specific product lines, and when issues are subsequently made from the raw materials stores to the production workshops they can be identified and charged to the appropriate cost accounts by the use of part numbers and job numbers. The procedures for relating such actual usage to the quantities which were adopted as standard usage allowances when preparing the original specification on which the quotation to the customer was based are explained in greater detail in Chapter 14.

As with direct materials, so the problem of allocating direct labour costs to the appropriate cost centre does not normally present significant problems. The accounting processes will merely require that the payroll should be analysed on a departmental or similar basis according to the way in which the direct labour cost information is required to be presented. Similarly to materials, the efficiency of direct labour usage expressed as a relationship between cost and output when compared with the standard usage factors adopted in the customer's quotation will be analysed and presented in the standard costing statements.

The costing procedures for allocating and recovering overheads expenditure present rather more complex problems, principally because, by definition, these items are not readily attributed to specific products or jobs. Such items as supervisory salaries, inspection, waiting time, holiday pay, etc, can usually be allocated to the departments or cost centres to which they relate, but it is probable that they cannot be more closely identified with the individual product lines which flow through these centres. Similarly, with such types of expenditure as rent, rates, power, etc, it is usually possible to apportion these costs to the departments concerned on an equitable basis, but thereafter they cannot be more closely attributed to the individual production cost centres. Overheads expense items such as insurances, managerial salaries, stores wages and production control costs are often of too general application to permit accurate allocation to individual departments and so they are of an even more indirect nature.

However, despite the difficulties of allocating these various types of overheads expenditure to their primary cost centres and subsequently to individual products or product lines, certain decisions as to the basis of apportionment, albeit of an arbitrary nature, must be made so as to enable overhead recovery rates to be fixed. The following is an elementary example of the type of allocation schedule that would be produced for an imaginary factory which has three main production departments and a tool room that provides services to two of the departments (B and C) in the estimated ratio of 2:1.

BUDGETED FACTORY OVERHEADS
Year to December 31st

Expense	Total £	A £	B £	C £	Tool room £
Rent and rates	8,000	3,000	2,000	2,000	1,000
Inspection	4,000	1,500	1,500	1,000	—
Power and Light	6,000	2,000	1,000	2,000	1,000
Supervision	4,000	1,000	500	1,500	1,000
Management	6,000	2,500	1,500	1,000	1,000
Other expenses	10,000	3,500	2,500	2,000	2,000
	38,000	13,500	9,000	9,500	6,000
Tool room allocation 2:1	—	—	4,000	2,000	—
	38,000	13,500	13,000	11,500	—
Direct Labour Payroll	25,000	10,000	8,000	7,000	—

In an allocation schedule of this nature, items such as rent and rates, supervision, etc, will be apportioned according to relative floor areas in the former case and actual cost centres in the latter. Other expenditure which cannot be allocated in this way will have to be apportioned on an appropriate estimated basis.

Having produced a departmental cost centre overheads expenditure allocation of this nature, the next stage is to decide on a basis for allocating the departmental expenditure to individual products or product lines. There are several recognized bases for allocating expenditure in this way and probably one of the most widely used is that known as the 'percentage on direct labour' method. This method relates the departmental overhead allocation to the direct labour payroll and expresses it as a percentage. In the above example the relative percentages are as follows:

Department A £13,500/£10,000 = 135%
Department B £13,000/£8,000 = 162%
Department C £11,500/£7,000 = 164%

With this method of overhead allocation, an overhead oncost, calculated on the direct labour content at the appropriate percentage rate, will be added to the other components of cost to give the total factory cost, viz:

	p
Materials	50
Labour	
Dept. A	25
Dept. B	75
Overheads	
Dept. A – 135%	34
Dept. B – 162%	121½
Factory Cost	305½

The disadvantage of this method is that the overhead oncost added to each unit of output will vary in relation to the labour cost element rather than the time element. As many items of overhead expenditure accrue on a time basis it might be more relevant to allocate oncost according to the labour time factor.

An alternative method of calculating oncost which takes account of the argument put forward above is that known as the labour/hour rate. The principle is very similar to the percentage on direct labour method except that the oncost is expressed in relation to the budgeted total labour hours to be worked in the year and an appropriate works oncost per unit is based on the labour time element in the individual unit of output. Thus, in the case of Department A in the above example, assuming that the shop had a direct labour force of 10 men, each of whom was expected to work 40 hours a week for 50 weeks in the year, the total productive hours would be 10 × 40 × 50 = 20,000 hours. Expressed as a labour/hour rate, this will give an oncost rate calculated as follows:

£13,500/20,000 hours @ 67½p per labour hour

Oncost will therefore be added to the factory cost of the individual unit of output* at the rate of 67½p per hour of direct labour time (or pro rata).

These two methods of allocating overheads to the individual unit of production are most suitable where labour constitutes a major element of the production process. Where this is the case, the amount of labour included in the unit cost is an indication of the relative

* The unit of output in this context means the unit of production or sales which is customary in the particular trade, eg singles, dozens, grosses, thousands, etc.

amount of time spent in passing through the production workshop, and with most overhead expenditure representing a function of time it is possible to obtain a reasonably equitable apportionment by relating it to the amount of labour content.

However, where the manufacturing processes are of a highly-automated nature and the direct labour element represents only a minor factor in the total cost structure, it is sometimes necessary to adopt an alternative method which is not dependent on the labour cost element. In these circumstances a more suitable basis of allocation is that known as the machine/hour rate. This method entails treating the machine which is carrying out the operation or operations as a cost centre and allocating thereto a proportion of the various items of shop overheads which have to be recovered from output. Thus, if the shop or machine room contains (say) six milling machines and four lathes, then such items as rent, rates, supervision, setting, power, maintenance, etc, would be apportioned to the machines on a suitable basis to give an annual overhead burden to be borne by each of them. Appropriate hourly overheads recovery rates would then be determined and applied to the work produced from each machine.

The example on page 118 illustrates the method of calculating machine/hour rates for a small machine shop:

By applying these hourly rates pro rata to work which is put on to these machines, the total shop overhead burden will be recovered over the year – assuming, of course, that the expected utilization rate is achieved by each machine.

	Total	Machine			
		1	2	3	4
	£	£	£	£	£
Rent and rates	5,000	1,250	1,250	1,250	1,250
Power and light	4,000	1,200	1,000	1,000	800
Supervision	1,400	350	350	350	350
Setting	2,000	600	600	400	400
Indirect materials	800	200	200	200	200
Maintenance	1,600	600	400	300	300
Other charges	1,800	500	400	400	500
	16,600	4,700	4,200	3,900	3,800
Annual running time (hours)		3,840	3,750	2,800	2,800
Machine hour rate		£1·22 per hr	£1·12 per hr	£1·39 per hr	£1·36 per hr
Machine operator's hourly rate		50p	50p	50p	50p

SELLING, DISTRIBUTION AND ADMINISTRATION EXPENSES

The methods of overhead recovery which have been described above are normally applicable only to those categories of expenditure which are customarily grouped under the general classification of factory (or works) overheads and they are not usually applied to the selling, distribution and administration expenses of the business.

The latter categories of expenditure are usually of a more indirect nature and are less easily identifiable as relating to specific products or activities. The method of recovery is therefore of a much more arbitrary nature and often consists of little more than applying a flat percentage oncost to the works cost or the conversion cost* of the product.

It must be emphasized, of course, that with all costing information which includes expenditure that has been allocated or apportioned on an estimated basis, the resulting 'costs' must be treated circumspectly, particularly when using such information in a competitive pricing situation. Such data obviously incorporates a number of assumptions as to the incidence of fixed costs and other expenditure of an indirect nature and ignores the true incidence of marginal costs, an explanation of which is given in Chapter 15.

---

* Conversion cost is the total of the direct labour and factory overheads element of the unit cost of the product, ie the 'added value' which has been incurred at the manufacturing stage.

CHAPTER FOURTEEN

Standard Costing

Just as the broader aspect of financial planning and control can be exercised through a carefully prepared trading budget, so the process can be extended in scope and detail to give similar control over the day-to-day manufacturing activities through a system of standard costing.

Although standard costing is sometimes thought to be a relatively complicated financial technique, it is, in essence, quite straightforward and capable of being applied in a wide variety of circumstances. It seeks to measure operating performance by comparing actual achievement against predetermined standards which have been accepted as representing a fair yardstick by which it should be judged.

Indeed, the most important part of a standard costing system is the creation of the cost standards which provide the basis of the control structure. In practice, of course, many companies already produce this information as a matter of routine, even though they may not be operating a standard costing system. Whenever a company's management prepares a quotation when tendering for a contract, it will usually produce a detailed schedule of cost estimates setting out materials requirements in the form of specifications, prices, quantities, scrap allowances, labour costs expressed in terms of wage rates, job timings, and relevant oncosts to provide for the necessary recovery of overheads expenses.

These estimates represent the management's best assessment of the performance standards that can reasonably be expected in fulfilment of the customer's requirements and can therefore be regarded as the yardstick by which subsequent achievement should be measured.

The costing procedures by which actual performances are evaluated will vary according to the nature and special characteristics of the individual industry but the principal requirement is that divergences from standard should be identified according to their nature under a number of distinct categories. It is customary to refer to such divergences from standard cost as 'variances' and the generally accepted categories are as follows:

Materials	– Price
	– Usage
Labour	– Rates of pay
	– Efficiency
Variable Overheads	– Expenditure
Fixed Overheads	– Expenditure
	– Capacity

For the purpose of illustration, it is assumed that the following quotation has been prepared as the basis for a contract tender and to serve as the subsequent standard cost.

QUOTATION PER 100 UNITS

MATERIALS	£
4 lb moulding power @ 12½p per lb	0·50
Bought out pressing @ 60p per 100	0·60
Total Materials	1·10

QUOTATION PER 100 UNITS (*cont.*)

	£
LABOUR	
Press operator – 15 mins @ 35p per hr	0·09
Assembly – 45 mins @ 25p per hr	0·19
Total Labour	0·28
WORKS OVERHEADS	
Variable – 100 per cent of labour	0·28
Fixed – 15p per 100 (based on 133 units per hour)	0·15
Total Works Overheads	0·43
Manufacturing Cost	1·81
SELLING, DISTRIBUTION AND ADMINISTRATION	
100 per cent of conversion cost (labour and overheads)	0·71
TOTAL COST	2·52
Profit – 10 per cent on total cost	0·25
SELLING PRICE (per 100)	2·77

Total quantity – 10,000

A costing system which was not based on standard costing methods would simply show the total costs incurred during the run, viz:

	£
Materials	111·60
Labour	26·28
Overheads	
Fixed	16·00
Variable	29·00
S.D. & A.	71·00
	253·88

However, information presented in this way is only of limited value as it gives no indication as to whether these costs are favourable or unfavourable compared with the standards on which the quoted price of £2·77 per 100 was based.

A standard costing system would segregate any divergences from these predetermined standards according to the nature of the factors which have brought them about and the following example shows how the variances arising in the above production run might be presented in standard costing form.

		£
SALES (at standard selling price)		
10,000 @ £2·77 per 100		277·00
Less Standard cost – 10,000		
@ £2·52 per 100		252·00
Standard Profit		25·00
Variances	£	
Materials		
Usage	3·75 Loss	
Price	2·15 Gain	
Labour		
Efficiency	1·95 Gain	
Rates of pay	0·23 Loss	
Overheads		
Fixed		
Expenditure	2·00 Loss	
Volume	1·00 Gain	
Variable		
Expenditure	1·00 Loss	1·88
Actual Profit		23·12

The variances thus disclosed are attributable to the following factors:

MATERIALS

Usage – An additional 30 lb of moulding powder was used during the production run causing an adverse variance.

$$30 \text{ lb @ } 12\tfrac{1}{2}\text{p} – £3·75 \text{ Loss}$$

Price – The buyer succeeded in purchasing the materials from an alternative source, thereby obtaining a price reduction of ½p per lb.

$$430 \text{ lb @ } \tfrac{1}{2}\text{p per lb} – £2·15 \text{ Gain}$$

LABOUR

Efficiency – Although the total standard time allowance for the assembly operations was 75 hours (45 mins per 100), the work was completed in 70 hours.

$$5 \text{ hours @ } 25\text{p per hour} – £1·25$$

Similarly, the pressing operations were completed in 2 hours under the standard time allowance of 25 hours (15 mins per 100).

$$2 \text{ hours @ } 35\text{p per hour} – £0·70$$

Total efficiency variance £1·95 Gain

Rates of pay – The rate of pay of the press operator was 36p per hour compared with the standard time rate of 35p per hour.

$$23 \text{ hours @ } 1\text{p} – £0·23 \text{ Loss}$$

OVERHEADS

Expenditure – The fixed overhead expenditure was budgeted at £15 but actual costs were £17.

Expenditure £2·00 Loss

Volume – Recovery of the budgeted fixed overhead was based on a production rate of 133 units per hour (a total time of 75 hours) but the actual rate achieved

was 143 per hour – showing an efficiency variance
of 5 hours.

5 hours @ 133 per hour = 665 @ 15p per 100
Volume £1·00 Gain

Expenditure – the variable overheads had been
budgeted at 28p per 100 (100 per cent of Direct
Labour) but actual expenditure was incurred at the
rate of 29p per 100.

10,000 @ 1p per 100 – £1·00 Loss

When the costing information is presented in this
form it is possible to obtain a much clearer idea of the
way in which performance compares with the estimates
on which price quotations have been based and
managers are able to concentrate their attention on
those aspects of production which are the cause of
excessive costs.

The mechanics of collecting and analysing this information does, of course, entail rather more clerical
work than the straightforward aggregation of expenditure under the broad categories of materials,
labour and overheads, but the additional control which
results will usually justify the extra cost.

Indeed, by careful planning of the accounting system,
much of the analysis work can be incorporated in the
day-to-day routine. Materials price variances arising at
the time of purchase can be isolated at the point where
suppliers' invoices are first recorded in the appropriate
accounts, and similarly labour rate variances can be
analysed at the point when the payroll is being made
up in the wages department. Efficiency variances will,
of course, be evaluated from the production information
which normally emanates from a factory's production
control department and expenditure variances can be

determined by the accounts department's own budget records.

Standard costing information can offer a very valuable tool to managers and if acted upon promptly and intelligently will do much to reduce unnecessary losses and wastage.

CHAPTER FIFTEEN

Costs and Prices

Although several books have been published in recent years devoted specifically to the subject of product pricing, subsequent legislative and economic developments have brought about a considerable change in the industrial environment that might well have rendered obsolete the conventional principles which form the basis for much of our current thinking on this subject.

However, any attempt at formulating a rational price structure must be founded on the observance of certain basic ground rules, foremost among them being the need to bear in mind the business's minimum financial objective of earning sufficient revenue to cover all costs, to service the capital employed, and to provide a surplus which, after providing for taxation, will ensure a modest contribution towards the financing of normal expansion requirements.

Although there are sometimes sound commercial reasons for pricing certain products at an apparently uneconomic level, this is a policy that must be conducted with particular care and can only be successful if, in the long run, the other products earn a sufficient margin to ensure an adequate contribution to the overheads and profits which have been sacrificed on the cut-price lines.

The multi-product company has considerably greater scope for developing a flexible price structure than has the firm with a restricted range of products, but despite this wider room for manoeuvre, every unit price calculation must include the variable costs which are incurred in that particular production line. Unless proper provision is made for the full recovery of incremental costs in individual unit prices, the end result can only be a drain on the firm's resources.

However, one of the major problems of pricing policy is to ensure that the overall margins across the full range of products are, in total, sufficient to yield a gross surplus that will cover all the selling, distribution and administrative overheads and leave an adequate margin of profit.

The conventional approach to price formulation is to prepare an estimate on costing lines to include the materials, direct labour and works overheads content of the product and to add a predetermined oncost to cover the administrative and other overheads and profit. Whilst this may result in a perfectly acceptable price schedule, it is equally likely that it could result in some products being needlessly under-priced while others may be over-priced.

So often the cost-accountant's approach creates an impression that the cost of a product, and consequently its price, is capable of precise definition, whereas in fact the price in many situations is what the customer is prepared to pay for the product. That part of the cost build-up which consists of an allocation of a portion of the firm's fixed overheads is, in most instances, a fairly arbitrary figure which when analysed can often be criticized as unduly burdening certain products and product lines with more than their fair share of the total cost.

The methods of allocating overhead expenses are dealt with in an earlier chapter and it will suffice at this stage to observe that the apportioning of fixed overheads to individual products is very much a matter of cost accounting convention. While it can form a very useful starting point from which to prepare a pricing schedule, there is much to commend a more flexible approach that takes greater account of market opportunities rather than accepting a slavish devotion to the conventional formula. However, no price structure can ignore the necessity for ensuring that, taken overall, provision is made for the full recovery of overheads over the planned sales volume.

The financial technique known as marginal costing seeks to apply this distinction between variable and fixed overheads costs to situations where a business is seeking to obtain work at a time when its factory is operating at an uneconomically low level of production because of a lack of orders. To the extent that the management is able to obtain work at prices which are in excess of the directly variable expenses relative to the particular product (ie materials, direct labour, packing materials, power, and other variable overheads), the surplus so earned is a contribution towards the fixed overheads of the business and thus the ultimate trading loss will be that much less than it would otherwise have been.

EXAMPLE

The company's fixed overheads amount to £500,000 (ie those overheads such as rent, rates, etc, which do not normally increase or decrease according to the volume of production). Its management succeeds in obtaining an order for 250,000 units at a selling price of £3·50 each. The cost structure of the product is as follows:

	£
Materials	1.00
Direct labour	0·75
Variable overheads and packing	1·37½
	3·12½
Fixed overheads	1·12½
Total cost (excluding profit)	4·25

By accepting the order at a selling price of £3·50 the company recovers all its variable expenditure and also earns a contribution of 37½p per unit towards its fixed overheads costs – a total contribution of £9,375 from the full order of 25,000 units.

However, marginal cost pricing does entail the acceptance of certain risks. While the firm in this example would stand to gain from adopting this policy at a time when the alternative was to have resources lying idle, there remains the danger that by letting it be known that it is cutting prices, the way is open for existing customers to press for price reductions against their own orders. Furthermore, by filling its spare capacity with cut-price work, the firm is placing itself in a position whereby it is precluded from tendering for more remunerative contracts if the opportunity should arise. Eventually, of course, even this cut-price work must be replaced by more profitable contracts, but the task of raising prices to a more economic level will made be all the more difficult by having to start from such a low base.

Very often, special factors need to be taken into consideration when formulating prices. Research expenditure and development costs are typical of this category and in certain circumstances special design characteristics and other similar features may well justify including an additional premium in the price structure.

In the last resort, of course, the decision as to the right price for the product may depend as much on the instinct of the sales manager as the expertise of the cost accountant, but their skills are complementary rather than competitive.

CHAPTER SIXTEEN

The Control of Capital Expenditure

Decisions which involve the authorization of capital expenditure projects are among the most important ones which face boards of directors and their managerial advisers. Most capital expenditure schemes entail the permanent commitment of relatively large sums of money over a number of years and according to the nature of the project there may be little chance of reversing a decision or making fundamental alterations once the proposal has reached the stage of advanced construction or contractual obligation.

Many faulty business decisions, such as an unsuitable managerial appointment or a commitment to manufacture a product which does not fulfil expectations, can often be retrieved before irreparable damage has been done, but once money has been spent on the acquisition of specialized plant for a project which shows no sign of meeting its budget targets, there is often little alternative but to invest yet more capital in the hope that a profit will eventually accrue. With some schemes it may be that the fundamentally uneconomic nature of their operation does not become apparent until the plant has been operating for some months, by which time, of course, considerable sums of working capital may have been lost in financing the early losses.

To shut down the plant at such a time may entail writing off much of the original capital expenditure, particularly if the machinery is of a specialized nature and consequently having a negligible resale value, while the prospect of allowing it to continue to run at a loss in the hope that the problems will eventually be overcome may be equally unpalatable.

These hazards alone are sufficient reason for managements to pay particular attention to the yardsticks which they use to evaluate and assess the prospective profitability of such projects.

The criterion which should apply when considering new capital expenditure proposals is the effect they will have on the ultimate profitability of the company as reflected in the rate of return earned by the capital funds which are employed in the business.

However, not every project which might come up for consideration can be assessed by this strict discipline of the contribution it makes in financial terms to the prosperity of the business. Many large firms consider that such intangible assets as staff loyalty and welfare might well be strengthened by the allocation of capital funds for the purpose of acquiring sports grounds or other welfare amenities that will yield no measurable return on the funds which are so employed. Similarly, the acquisition of additional distribution facilities by opening new warehouses or bulk distribution centres may, in the short term, show no benefits in the profit and loss account which can be put forward as the justification for incurring the expenditure. It may be that the ultimate benefits of such a project will be postponed for several years, although the execution of the scheme is an essential prerequisite to the longer term expansion of the business.

Such projects will, of course, have to be assessed by more subjective criteria than would be applied to most capital expenditure proposals, but in this chapter we are primarily concerned with those schemes which form the majority of capital spending plans and which are usually capable of being assessed by the more orthodox standards of the return they are expected to yield on the funds which will be required to finance them.

PAY-BACK PERIOD

The pay-back period method of assessment is one that is widely used and finds a general acceptance among businessmen because it justifies a project in terms of the length of time during which the original capital outlay is at risk. The calculation is made as follows:

Cost of machine	– £25,000
Annual profit or cost saving	– £5,000
Cost/pay-back period	– 5 years

While this method does take account of the rate at which the resulting cash flows provide for the recovery of the capital expended, it suffers from the disadvantage that it ignores the profits which accrue in later years. Thus, it appears to favour a project which shows a quick return of capital, whereas an alternative proposal which entails a slower build up of profits but shows good returns in later years may in consequence be turned down. This is illustrated by the following competing proposals:

	Project A	Project B
Cost of proposal	£15,000	£15,000
Estimated cash flow	£	£
Year 1	5,000	1,000
Year 2	6,000	4,000
Year 3	5,000	6,000
Year 4	3,000	6,000
Year 5	2,000	5,000
Year 6	1,000	4,000
	22,000	26,000

The pay-back period method would favour Project A, whereas taken over the six-years period the balance of advantage might well lie in favour of Project B.

However, there are circumstances in which it is a perfectly adequate method of assessment and it meets the requirements of simplicity of application.

RETURN ON AVERAGE CAPITAL EMPLOYED

The return on capital employed method does attempt to take account of the profits which accrue over the life of the project, although making no adjustment for the relative rate at which they are earned, viz:

A project is estimated to cost £25,000 and to have a useful working life of 10 years. The profit yield has been calculated at £1,000 in the first year, £2,500 in the following five years, and £1,500 per year thereafter.

Average capital employed £12,500
Total profit over 10 years £19,500
Average annual profit £1,950

$$\text{Rate of return} = \frac{£1,950}{£12,500} = 15 \cdot 6 \text{ per cent}$$

While this method does express the profit as a rate of return on capital employed, it places no greater relative value on £1 earned in the first year than on £1 earned in the tenth year.

DISCOUNTED CASH FLOW

The discounted cash flow (DCF) technique of project appraisal has come into favour in recent years and shows considerable advantages over the other methods because it attempts to apply more objective yardsticks to the task of assessing proposals. To some extent it

combines the best features of the pay-back and rate of
return methods but also embodies added refinements
which seek to evaluate the timing of the cash flows.

It necessitates preparing a detailed year by year
estimate of the cash inflows and outflows and then discounting them back to their present value at such rate
of interest as will produce a total discounted value equal
to the estimated capital cost of the project. The following simple example will illustrate the principle:

A proposal has been submitted for a plant installation that will require a capital outlay of £27,000. The
estimated annual net cash flow over the period, when
discounted back at 9 per cent, produces a discounted
value of £26,901 and this being an acceptable rate, the
project is put in hand, viz:

Year	Net cash flow	Discounting factor	Present value
	£		£
1	1,000	0·917431	917
2	2,500	0·841680	2,104
3	8,000	0·772183	6,177
4	10,000	0·708425	7,084
5	9,000	0·649931	5,849
6	8,000	0·596267	4,770
	38,500		26,901

The arithmetic for such a calculation is based on the
compound interest principle and is not difficult to apply,
although the adjustments which have to be made to
allow for investment grants and other capital expenditure incentive schemes do sometimes add to the complexity of the workings.

The method aims to ascertain the rate of interest

(profit) which must be obtained on the future income streams to produce, at their present values, the equivalent of the present capital cost of the investment.

The technique is sometimes criticized for its relative complexity of calculation and also because it requires an estimate of profits over a future period of years which must, of necessity, be of diminishing validity. However, the fact that the calculations are complex is not a valid argument for not adopting a technique and the directors will certainly assign the detail work to experts who are experienced in this aspect of project evaluation. Regarding the problems of forward forecasting, these will arise whichever method of assessment is used and this cannot therefore be regarded as a serious argument against the use of DCF methods.

Undoubtedly the increased amount of attention devoted to these techniques has encouraged managements to subject investment proposals to a rather more critical and searching examination than they might otherwise have done, and to this extent their increasing use is to be welcomed as bringing a more objective approach to the task of assessing projects.

However, because of the considerable amount of literature that has been produced on the subject of DCF over recent years, there is a danger that over-exposure to the refined mathematics which is sometimes introduced into these writings tends to invest the whole exercise with an unwarranted air of precision which is rarely justified by the facts.

The real worth of an investment proposal lies in the credibility of the forecasts of sales demand and production capacity which underpin the validity of the assessment, and any miscalculation or misjudgement of these factors is likely to be of far greater consequence than the relatively marginal effects of errors caused by, for example, the use of a wrong rate of interest in the discounting calculations. Probably the principal virtue of the DCF technique lies in the way in which it ranks competing projects according to the timing of their cash flows. Thus, supposing that in addition to the project quoted in the above example, there had been put forward an alternative project which also required a capital outlay of £27,000 but which had a different pattern of anticipated cash flows. By applying the same rate of interest and discounting these annual cash flows back to their present value, it is possible to make a comparative assessment that will assist the management in deciding which of the two projects to back, viz:

Year	Net cash flow	Discounting factor	Present value
	£		£
1	2,000	0·917431	1,834
2	4,500	0·841680	3,788
3	10,000	0·772183	7,722
4	9,000	0·708425	6,376
5	7,000	0·649931	4,549
6	6,000	0·596267	3,578
	38,500		27,847

It will be seen that as a result of the cash flows from this project emerging at an earlier stage in the time span of the assessment period, the present value, using the same interest rate of 9 per cent, is slightly higher than that of the first proposal. Other things being equal, the second project would be chosen because it yields a slightly higher return, but it must again be emphasized that when trading forecasts are made for as far as five or six years ahead, they cannot be regarded as giving more than a general indication of the probable degree of profitability over that period. Recent experience of national economic planning must surely have caused even the most ardent exponent of forward forecasting to have reservations about the validity of long term projections.

All forward forecasting is based on data which represents a distillation of the opinions of experts, be they marketing managers, production engineers, accountants or economists, and it must inevitably incorporate a degree of bias as represented by the optimism or pessimism of the person who has contributed to its preparation. If, for example, an engineer is preparing forward estimates of production from a proposed installation which he intends to advocate to the board of directors, then it is a perfectly human reaction that he should inject some of his own optimism into his recommendations, thereby possibly putting the forecast in an unduly favourable light.

Where a project requires only a small capital outlay, it is hardly worthwhile going to the trouble of preparing a DCF calculation and very often the decision will be fairly obvious from the information which is given in support of the application.

In the case of proposals which cannot be assessed according to the criteria of return on capital invested, such as welfare facilities, improvements to roads and services, etc, it is necessary to ensure that once the relevant expenditure has been authorized, it is subject to strict budgeting control to ensure that outlays are kept within the agreed limits.

Indeed, it is vital to the success of any project that expenditure should be rigidly controlled throughout the construction and installation period, for any additional costs which were not contemplated when making the original evaluation will inevitably have the effect of reducing the rate of return which can be expected from it when it becomes operational.

CHAPTER SEVENTEEN

The Control of Working Capital

The nature of the principal items which normally comprise a business's working capital have been discussed in previous chapters but we must now consider in more detail the techniques which have been evolved to assist managements to exercise control over their use of working capital resources.

Although most decisions relating to the investment of working capital can, if subsequently proved faulty, often be reversed at very much less cost than can corresponding decisions involving investment of capital in buildings, plant, machinery or similar fixed assets, nevertheless the misuse of such funds may prove to be extremely costly. Losses may arise from the investment of working capital in trading stocks that are subsequently rendered obsolete, and inadequate credit control can cause large sums to be unnecessarily immobilized in the financing of credit to customers.

When new projects are being planned entailing an expansion of business activity, in the same way that the proposed investment of funds in capital projects must be forecasted and evaluated in terms of the return on capital employed, so the corresponding working capital requirements must be assessed so that the overall investment can be evaluated.

Thus, supposing that a new project which is being planned reveals the following prospective sales, purchases and stock, on a month by month basis:

	Month 1 £	Month 2 £	Month 3 £	Month 4 £	Month 5 £
Sales	50,000	60,000	65,000	70,000	80,000
Purchases	50,000	50,000	50,000	50,000	45,000
Stocks	100,000	110,000	120,000	140,000	140,000

Assuming that the average period of credit taken by customers is two months and that a similar period of credit is granted by suppliers, the net flow of cash would be as follows:

	Month 3 £	Month 4 £	Month 5 £	Month 6 £	Month 7 £
Cash Inflow					
Sales	50,000	60,000	65,000	70,000	80,000
Cash Outflow					
Purchases	50,000	50,000	50,000	50,000	45,000
Wages	5,000	5,000	5,500	6,000	6,000
Overheads	10,000	10,000	10,000	10,500	11,000
	65,000	65,000	65,500	66,500	62,000
Net Cash Flow	15,000—	5,000—	500—	3,500+	18,000+
Cumulative Cash Flow	15,000—	20,000—	20,500—	17,000—	1,000+
Trading Stocks	120,000	140,000	140,000	150,000	150,000

It will be seen that during the early months of the expansion period there was a heavy commitment of working capital as trading stocks were built up in readiness for the sales expansion which followed towards the end of the period. On the assumption that the level of sales and purchases in Month 7 represents the high point of the expansion period, the new working capital requirement could be calculated as follows:

	£
Trading stocks (materials and finished goods)	150,000
Trade debtors (2 months sales)	150,000
	300,000
Less: Trade creditors (2 months purchases)	95,000
	205,000
Other commitments (say)	45,000
	£250,000

Thus the overall working capital requirement by Month 7 would be approximately £250,000. In practice, of course, not all of this capital would be raised in cash and on the basis of a sound forward estimate which can be supported by a healthy order book, the business ought to be able to raise at least part of its additional working capital needs by means of an overdraft facility from its bankers.

One of the financial perils which has to be guarded against during a period of expansion is that of over-trading. Smaller-sized firms that do not undertake any formal financial planning, or perhaps do not even have a proper system of financial control, sometimes enter into a period of rapid expansion without taking any steps to secure access to the additional working capital resources which they will almost certainly need. The build up of stocks and the commitment of considerable sums of capital to finance customers' credit, when coupled with corresponding demands to meet payments to creditors for increased purchases which had been made in anticipation of the expanded need for production materials, combine to place a great strain on the business's working capital resources.

In such circumstances there is a danger that the business will over-stretch its cash resources and find itself in the position where its bankers and its larger suppliers are unwilling to give further credit. Should the bank decide to refuse further borrowing facilities, the fact that the business is in difficulties because of lack of working capital will quickly become apparent to its creditors, with the consequence that they will start pressing for early payment of their accounts and thus compound the business's troubles. This situation will persist until the expansion has slowed down, but even when a plateau has been reached there will still be a need for a working margin greater than that which sufficed before the boom began.

Firms operating in trades or industries which are largely of a seasonal character (farming or firework manufacture are typical examples) will often experience temporary cash shortages, particularly as they approach their peak selling months, but because this situation can usually be foreseen and will normally be resolved when the accumulated stocks are run down, it is not difficult to obtain temporary bank loan facilities to tide over the period of cash scarcity.

CREDIT CONTROL

One of the most important aspects of maintaining adequate working capital resources is to ensure that the total amount of debt outstanding in the form of short term credit granted to customers on monthly account is kept under close surveillance.

During the time which elapses between despatching goods to the customer from the warehouse and receiving cash in settlement of the invoiced value, the working capital thus employed is temporarily outside the control of the supplier and it is therefore essential that effective credit control procedures should be used to reduce the possibility of financial difficulties brought about by the action of the company's own customers. In the case of firms that normally allow their customers a month's credit on purchases, this means that in practice the minimum average period of credit will be one and a half months. Invoices are usually required to be paid within one month of the end of the month in which the goods are delivered and it follows that some will be outstanding for a bare month and others will be almost two months old before they are due for settlement. However, should several major customers delay payment of their accounts by one month or more, then very soon the business may find that the total sum of working capital tied up in the form of debts has shown a marked increase, to the detriment of its ability to pay its own suppliers' accounts.

This problem of restricting the period of credit allowed to customers is very much more pressing than the possibility that some of them may default completely, as with average care and caution the bad debts problem should normally remain within acceptable limits. Unfortunately, delays in settlement of accounts are a commonplace financial management dilemma and even some of the largest companies are used to taking two or more months' credit on their suppliers' accounts. The methods of persuasion and coercion that are sometimes used to get slow-paying customers to keep their accounts up to date are outside the scope of this book, but we should briefly consider the use that can be made of the available financial information as a means of exercising broad control over the total amount of customers' debt.

By expressing this figure of total debt as a proportion of turnover and comparing any relative change from month to month it soon becomes apparent if there is a tendency for the average period of credit to show an undue increase. The following example illustrates the application of this simple but effective check procedure.

	July	August	September	October	November	December
	£	£	£	£	£	£
Sales	55,000	60,000	58,000	64,000	52,000	65,000
Debtors			146,000	142,000	146,000	147,000

The total monthly balance on debtors' accounts is expressed as a proportion of the total sales for the most recent three months sales period, viz:

	£
Debtors at December	147,000
December sales	65,000
	82,000
November sales	52,000
	30,000

Balance as proportion of October sales $\dfrac{30,000}{64,000} = \cdot 47$

Therefore total debt = 2·47 months

A similar calculation based on the debtors' balances at November will show the following position:

	£
Debtors at November	146,000
November sales	52,000
	94,000
October sales	64,000
	30,000

Balance as proportion of September sales $\dfrac{30,000}{58,000} = \cdot52$

Therefore total debt $= 2\cdot52$ months

The comparative position over the four months is as follows:

	September	October	November	December
Total debt in months	2·51	2·33	2·52	2·47

This indicator reveals that debts are being kept at a reasonably consistent relationship of two and a half months' sales and show no significant trend either to reduce or lengthen the average period of credit.

An alternative method of checking the trend of investment of funds in trade debts is to express the monthly total of balances in terms of Sales Days. Thus, if the company's annual rate of turnover is £1,500,000, this represents a Sales Value per Working Day (240 days per annum) of £1,500,000/240 = £6,250.

If the monthly total of debtors' balances is divided by this Sales Day value, the resulting ratio will, when compared from month to month, indicate any tendency for payments to slow down, viz:

	September £	October £	November £	December £
Debtors' Balances	468,000	500,000	480,000	456,000
Sales Days	75	80	77	73

With this method it may be advisable to recalculate the Sales Day value each month, based on the immediately preceding twelve months' sales, as any significant increase or decrease in the current trend may alter the Sales Day relationship to a material extent.

CONTROL OF STOCKS

To the extent that the level of stocks of raw materials and finished goods is entirely within the control of the business's management, this aspect of working capital investment would appear to present fewer problems than might be encountered with control of debtors. However, for many firms, particularly those with a fast production cycle rate, maintaining a satisfactory balance between the requirements of the production programme and the availability of working capital resources can call for highly developed stock control systems.

With the increasing application of computers and mathematical techniques to the problems of production planning and stock control, it is possible to plan deliveries of raw materials and bought in components according to rigidly programmed timetables, and this type of stock scheduling is seen at its most sophisticated level in the motor car industry where many essential supplies are delivered to the factory almost within hours of being fed to the production lines.

However, for many firms the use of such complex procedures would be beyond their administrative and financial resources and so they have to rely on rather more rudimentary techniques. A simple but quite useful rule of thumb check on the overall level of investment in raw materials stocks can be obtained by relating the monthly total of such stocks to the moving annual total* of raw materials purchases, viz:

* The Moving Annual Total of a series of monthly figures is obtained by taking the total of the immediately preceding twelve months' monthly figures. Thus, the total moves forward each month by adding the current month's figure and deducting the corresponding one for the same month of the previous year.

	Month 1	Month 2	Month 3	Month 4
Moving annual total of raw materials purchases	£325,000	£340,000	£338,000	£335,000
Raw materials stock	£52,000	£56,000	£55,000	£56,000
Stock/MAT ratio	1:6·25	1:6·07	1:6·15	1:5·98

It will be seen from this monthly ratio between raw materials stocks and raw materials purchases that it has deteriorated from 1:6·25 to 1:5·98, indicating a relative increase in the investment in such stocks.

Such a crude yardstick can at best be only a guide to the trend of stockholding and is not in itself conclusive evidence that stock levels are unduly high. However, it does highlight the broad movement of stocks and should put the manager on inquiry to carry out such further investigation as may be desirable. It does not, of course, give any indication as to whether the stock figure includes any obsolete items which might possibly be sold off, even if only for scrap, thereby releasing funds which can be more profitably used for other purposes.

This type of statistical check can also be applied to the control of finished goods stocks, with the ratio being calculated for the monthly figure of finished goods stocks against the moving annual total of sales.

CASH CONTROL

Just as adequate control must be maintained over customers' outstanding accounts so as to ensure that there is an adequate flow of cash to meet working capital needs, so it is possible that from time to time the business may find that its cash balance is temporarily in excess of immediate day to day requirements.

If these idle cash balances are allowed to remain on

current account for an extended period of time without earning interest, this will result in a dilution of the over-all rate of return on capital employed and would reflect on the management's ability to earn an adequate return on the capital resources entrusted to its care.

Depending on the length of time during which these funds are likely to be available for alternative employment, consideration should be given to the possibility of temporarily re-investing them with the objective of earning interest. If the period of inactivity is likely to be short, the funds might best be transferred to deposit account with the company's bankers where they can be quickly made available for return to working capital when required. Rather longer term investment for periods of two to three months might best be made in the form of purchases of Treasury Bills, thereby providing a marginally better rate of interest but still carrying a high degree of availability in the event of a sudden and unforeseen need for ready cash.

For periods in excess of three months, the funds could be placed on deposit with a reputable finance company or alternatively with a local authority. Such deposits would carry a considerably higher rate of interest but would obviously not be so readily available in the event of funds being required before the maturity date of the loans.

Longer term investment would become a matter of broader company policy and is therefore outside the scope of this chapter.

CREDITORS' ACCOUNTS

Although the monthly account credit facilities which are usually granted by suppliers are less obviously a source of working capital funds, they do in fact form a valuable supplement to the funds derived from more permanent sources.

Where a supplier has agreed to accept payment on normal monthly account terms, then clearly full advantage should be taken of this facility on the assumption that the prices at which the supplier's goods are bought make an appropriate allowance for the return on capital thus employed. Many firms do offer cash discounts of up to $2\frac{1}{2}$ per cent to customers who make prompt cash settlement within a specified time limit (probably 7–14 days), but before accepting such terms it is advisable to consider whether they offer a better return than might be gained by deferring payment to the full due date, thereby gaining the benefit of a correspondingly higher bank balance (or lower overdraft) during this period.

While this chapter has considered the problems and techniques of working capital control from the viewpoint of each of its principal constituent parts, in practice it requires a wider approach which views the business in its overall context. For example, although at a particular point in time the amount outstanding on creditors' accounts may seem unduly high, this position may be balanced by the impending receipt of a progress payment against a large contract. The fact that cash resources appear to be at a low ebb is not necessarily serious if the security provided by fixed assets assures adequate support from the company's bankers.

CHAPTER EIGHTEEN

Stock and Work in Progress

Although many managers who are not directly involved in the annual stocktaking tend to think of it as being a somewhat tiresome chore which is in some way connected with the preparation of the annual accounts, it does in fact form a vital part of the procedures by which a business ascertains its trading profit and establishes the value of that part of its working capital which is invested in raw materials, work in progress, and finished goods.

It was explained in an earlier chapter that when at the end of the financial year a business is holding stocks of materials which have been charged into purchases during that year, it is necessary to value those materials at their purchase price and to carry forward the value as a charge to the following period, thereby relieving the current period's accounts of charges which they should not be expected to bear. It will be seen that by making this adjustment for both opening and closing stocks, the correct charge against the year's revenue is thus established, viz:

	£
Opening stock at January 1st	15,000
Purchases (for year)	110,000
	125,000
Closing stock at December 31st	18,000
Materials consumed during year £107,000	

However, for those businesses whose manufacturing operations are of a complex nature this stocktaking exercise offers many problems which often require the application of considerable accounting expertise and judgement. Where the total sum thus invested represents a significant proportion of the year's output, even a relatively small proportionate error in valuation can make a substantial difference to the apparent figure of annual profit. Thus, using the example of a firm which has capital invested in the form of stock and work in progress representing approximately three months' work, the effect of a 5 per cent error in the valuation of the year-end inventory could result in an overstatement of 6 per cent in the figure of trading profit, viz:

		£	£
Sales			700,000
Direct Labour		96,000	
Materials		160,000	
Works Overheads		130,000	
		386,000	
Opening Stock	93,000		
Closing Stock	84,000		
Decrease in stock		9,000	395,000
Manufacturing Profit			305,000
Selling		60,000	
Distribution		95,000	
Administration		80,000	
			235,000
Trading Profit			£70,000

If it is assumed that because of the overvaluation of closing stocks they were overstated by £4,000, this would produce a corresponding error in the figure of trading profits. Thus, the correct profit for the year should have been £66,000 and not the figure of £70,000 as shown by the accounts.

Errors of this magnitude are not unknown and this example illustrates the importance of ensuring that the inventory is verified by an accurate stocktaking system and that the basis of valuation is according to principles that will produce a fair and reasonable result.

One of the particular problems which is frequently encountered when preparing the inventory arises when deliveries are made by the suppliers of raw materials during the last day or two of the financial year but for one reason or another they fail to render their invoice in sufficient time for it to be included in the year's purchases. Unless the system of internal checking is designed to draw attention to such a happening, there is a possibility that it would remain undetected with the consequence that the year's profit would be overstated accordingly.

Similarly, if a consignment of goods had been loaded into a delivery vehicle on the last day of the financial year in readiness for delivery to a customer the following day, the possibility may arise that the goods will neither be included in the year's sales nor in the figure of closing stock. The consequence of such an omission would be that the year's profit is thereby understated and the following year's results will be correspondingly overstated.

The valuation of stock and work in progress presents similar complex problems, in spite of the body of valuation principles which has been formulated in an endeavour to produce reasonably uniform accounting procedures.

In regard to the materials content of stock and work in progress, the generally accepted basis of pricing is 'cost or net realizable value, whichever is the lower'. In this context, cost means the original cost to the holder of the stock and net realizable value means the value which might be realized in the event of enforced sale, but within these broad definitions there are differing interpretations according to the custom of the trade or the particular circumstances of the individual firm.

Where the prices of stock items are subject to fluctuation the question arises as to the particular method which should be adopted for pricing out the issues from stock. If the individual items have a significant unit value, one of the methods of pricing in most common use is known as 'First In, First Out' (FIFO), based on the simple assumption that the oldest items of each type of stock are used first. This method has the virtue that it is correct in principle but suffers from the disadvantage that it can become complicated to apply in practice if the rate of stock turnover is high and the prices of purchases are subject to frequent changes.

An alternative method which overcomes some of the disadvantages of FIFO is that which is known as the average price method. This method entails calculating an average price for the total quantity of each type of item held in stock and pricing out all issues accordingly. Whenever a new batch of items is received in stock, it necessitates re-calculating the average price for application to subsequent issues, viz:

		£
Stock held	400 @ 17½p	70
	600 @ 16½p	100
	1,000 @ 17p	170
Issued	300 @ 17p	50
	700 @ 17p	120
Received	500 @ 18p	90
	1,200 @ 17½p	210
Issued	400 @ 17½p	70
Balance	800 @ 17½p	140

The advantage of the average price method is that it is equitable, comparatively easy to operate, and avoids the complications of the FIFO method.

Another method which is in common usage in the United Kingdom is known as the standard cost basis. This is based on the standard prices which are built up for use in conjunction with a standard costing system (see Chapter 14) and is ideally suited where the industry is one engaged in large volume production or a uniform process system.

A method known as 'Last In, First Out' (LIFO) is sometimes used in America but as it is not recognized for tax purposes in the United Kingdom it is not strictly relevant to our consideration of generally accepted accounting practices in this country.

In relation to the valuation of work in progress, it is this aspect of the preparation of annual or other periodic accounts that often provides some of the most difficult problems, depending, of course, on the nature of the products which are involved. In a highly complex process industry such as, for example, petrochemicals or oil refining, the valuation of by-products or those primary products which are at an intermediate conversion stage may involve reliance upon the expert assessment of chemists and other technically qualified personnel.

The basic elements of manufactured work in progress are materials, labour and overheads. The items which comprise work in progress at the year end will normally be grouped according to the various stages of manufacture reached at the close of business. The amount of materials and labour expended up to each stage of manufacture will normally be evaluated from standard cost schedules and the appropriate overhead oncost allocated according to the basis used.

There are wide variations in the treatment of overheads in stock and work in progress, ranging from exclusion of all overheads at one extreme to the inclusion of full overheads with the exception of selling, distribution and finance charges at the other. The effect of including an allocation of overheads in the valuation of work in progress is that a proportion of the expenditure represented thereby is carried forward to the succeeding accounting period and is thus charged against the revenue of the period in which the goods are eventually converted into sales. Probably the more common practice is to include at least a proportion of factory overheads in the work in progress valuation.

The higher the amount of working capital resources invested in trading stocks, relative to the total capital investment in the business and the size of the annual turnover, the greater is the need to ensure that the compilation and valuation of the inventory leaves little room for doubt as to its accuracy and soundness. As it has been demonstrated above, a comparatively small error may produce a disproportionate under- or over-statement of the annual profit which, if not detected at the time, will affect the accuracy of two years' accounts – those for which the inaccurate valuation provided the closing stock figure and also the succeeding period for which it formed the opening stock.

CHAPTER NINETEEN

Where has the Profit gone?

To the non-financial manager one of the most bewildering aspects of interpreting company accounts is relating the profits earned in the year to the business's ability to meet its capital expenditure and working capital commitments.

Often after the conclusion of a successful trading year the business appears to be suffering from a shortage of cash – a phenomenon which is not easily related to a period of prosperity.

The general nature of this problem so far as it affects working capital requirements is referred to in Chapter 17, but from the viewpoint of accounting presentation the conventional accounting documents – the balance sheet and the profit and loss account – are inadequate for the purpose of relating the movements of funds within the business to the cash flows which arise from profits on trading and other sources.

Within recent years some companies have amplified the information given in the statutory accounts by including an additional financial statement designed to bridge this gap in accounting presentation and the method which has been most favoured is the Sources and Applications of Funds statement.

The movement of funds within the business comprise the additional resources derived from trading profits (or the resources depleted by losses) and the capital movements which arise from share issues and other sources. The effect of these movements of funds within the business are, of course, recorded in the books of account but they only become apparent by making a comparative analysis of two successive balance sheets.

This can best be illustrated by making such a comparison based on the following balance sheets of an imaginary company:

BALANCE SHEETS AT DECEMBER 31st

	Year 1 £	Year 2 £	Increase/ Decrease £
Employment of Capital			
Freehold Premises	695,000	645,000	50,000—
Plant and Machinery	250,000	405,000	155,000+
Motor Vehicles	20,000	25,000	5,000+
	965,000	1,075,000	110,000+
Patents, Trade Marks etc	20,000	20,000	—
Investments			
Quoted	100,000	140,000	40,000+
Unquoted	40,000	40,000	—
Current Assets			
Stock and Work in Progress	420,000	540,000	120,000+
Debtors	967,000	885,000	82,000—
Treasury Bills	5,000	15,000	10,000+
Tax Reserve Certificates	50,000	70,000	20,000+
Cash	3,000	5,000	2,000+
	1,445,000	1,515,000	70,000+
Current Liabilities			
Creditors	390,000	410,000	20,000+
Bank Overdraft	61,000	80,000	19,000+
Taxation	35,000	51,000	16,000+
Proposed Dividends	54,000	54,000	—
	540,000	595,000	55,000+
Net Current Assets	905,000	920,000	15,000+
	£2,030,000	£2,195,000	£165,000+

Capital Employed	£	£	£
Share Capital			
Preference Shares – 7%	200,000	200,000	—
Ordinary Shares	800,000	800,000	—
	1,000,000	1,000,000	—
Capital Reserve	50,000	50,000	—
General Reserve	170,000	275,000	105,000+
Profit and Loss Account	69,000	45,000	24,000−
	1,289,000	1,370,000	81,000+
Unsecured Loan Stock	500,000	500,000	—
Taxation	51,000	75,000	24,000+
Minority Interests	190,000	250,000	60,000+
	£2,030,000	£2,195,000	£165,000+

The company's Profit and Loss Account for Year 2 was as follows:

		£
Trading profit		299,000
(After charging depreciation of £105,000 on fixed assets)		
Less: Corporation Tax		124,000
Profit after tax		175,000
Dividends:		
Preference – 7%	14,000	
Ordinary:		
Interim – 5%	40,000	
Final – 5%	40,000	
		94,000
Profit retained in business		£81,000

The third column of figures in this analysis of balance sheet figures shows the changes in the deployment of funds within the business between the two balance sheet dates. However, when presented in this way they are not particularly comprehensible and so they are customarily rearranged in the form of a Sources and Applications of Funds statement, of which the following is a typical example:

SOURCES AND APPLICATIONS OF FUNDS

Sources of Funds	£	£
Depreciation retentions		105,000
Trading profits	299,000	
Less: Corporation Tax	124,000	
		175,000
Increase in creditors (including Tax)		60,000
Increase in bank overdraft		19,000
Reduction of debtors		82,000
Increase in minority interests		60,000
		501,000
Applications of Funds		
Increases in fixed assets		215,000
Purchase of additional investments		40,000
Increase in stocks		120,000
Additional Treasury Bills and Tax Reserve Certificates		30,000
Increase in cash balance		2,000
Payments of dividends		94,000
		501,000

It will be seen from the first section of this statement that the sources of new funds include the cash retentions which arise from charging depreciation in the accounts and also any extension of credit given by suppliers.

The use of such a statement for the purpose of accounting presentation greatly facilitates the explanation of the movement of funds within the business and illustrates how the earning of profit is not necessarily accompanied by a corresponding increase in liquid cash resources.

Indeed, as has been illustrated in Chapter 17, a period of expansion in turnover and output is often accompanied by a shortage of cash resources, particularly where the expansion is preceded by a capital expenditure programme which is to be financed from existing resources and current earnings.

CHAPTER TWENTY

Management Ratio Schemes

The full value of statistical and financial information is only derived when it is used for the purpose of comparison with similar data relating to other time periods or activities. Current year's sales are compared with those of earlier years or forecasted figures for future periods; rates of return on capital employed are compared with those achieved in earlier years or the rates being earned by other companies in the same or similar industries; the potential profitability of a proposed new product line is compared with margins obtained on alternative or competing lines – thus the *raison d'être* of management information systems is to enable such comparisons to be made and the relevant conclusions to be drawn as the basis for subsequent decisions.

The production of the necessary data within the individual firm will not normally entail particular complications and the limiting factor is usually the cost of analysing the basic material when considered in terms of the amount of clerical labour or mechanical aids which the management considers is justified by the value to be derived from the end-product. The more sophisticated the accounting and statistical information is required to be by the demands of management, the more complex is the underlying system and the more the number of people who are required to operate it. Obviously, the extent and cost of the financial and statistical information produced within the firm must be weighed against the value derived therefrom, and any further extension must be justified from this base.

However, internally produced statistics represent only one source of potential management information and much of equal value can be gained by comparing performance against standards which have been derived from outside sources, although it is not normally possible to obtain such comparative information without privileged access to the accounts of other companies.

In response to this demand for a means of comparing financial performance against the results achieved by other companies in the same industry, a number of trade associations have over the years developed their own schemes for inter-firm comparison of information of this nature. The essential prerequisite of such a scheme is that the participating member firms are assured that the financial information relating to their own activities which they supply in support of their contribution should be treated in strict confidence and it is therefore essential that the officials or organization responsible for compiling and disseminating the inter-firm comparison figures should be seen to be independent, trustworthy and impartial.

Successful trade association schemes have flourished for some years and one of the pioneers was the British Federation of Master Printers which is now well established in this field. Other equally successful schemes have followed and they are becoming almost a status symbol for the more active trade associations which seek to provide their members with positive evidence of the benefits of membership.

Another organization which has made and continues to make a valuable contribution to the cause of inter-firm comparisons is the Centre for Interfirm Comparison

which was established in 1959 by the British Institute of Management in association with the British
Productivity Council. The Centre sets out to run such
schemes for those industries which are not already running their own trade association schemes and where
there is a sufficient degree of support from companies
within the industry to warrant the preparation of the
necessary statistical information.

Obviously the value to be derived from participation
in an inter-firm scheme is related to the accuracy and
amount of basic data which provides the raw material
for compiling this information. Furthermore, because of
wide variations in the accounting treatment adopted by
individual firms (the period(s) over which fixed assets
are depreciated provides just one example) and their
differing methods of financing their businesses, there
are bound to be problems of definition and non-com-
parability which must be adjusted for when providing
the relevant comparative information. Some firms will
choose to purchase the freeholds of their premises while
others will prefer to acquire a lease, which may be of
long or short term duration. The methods of financing
the acquisition of plant and machinery may also show
wide variations, with some firms preferring outright
purchase for cash while others may elect to enter
into hire purchase or leasing contracts (see also
Chapter 7).

However, despite the problems created by these varying methods of accounting treatment, a wide measure
of comparability has been achieved in practice and the
benefits of participation in a well-run scheme are not to
be denied. So far as criticism can be levelled at these
schemes, it is possibly that they produce an excess of
ratios and disperse management attention over too

wide an area – thus tending to distract attention from the relevant and essential index figures.

Undoubtedly the most interesting and most useful yardsticks for participating firms are the ratio of trading profit to capital employed and the ratio of trading profit to sales, but deriving from these basic performance standards there is a wide range of intermediate ratios which are of varying degrees of interest to the managers concerned.

Taking the example of the British Federation of Master Printers scheme as being representative of the more comprehensive type of exercise, the individual member firm is able to compare its own ratios, in the form in which they were prepared for compilation of the overall averages, with comparable average ratios of groups of firms within the scheme categorized according to their size. Within each of these size groups the average ratios are presented to show the lower quartile, the median and the upper quartile.* Thus, it is possible for the managements of individual firms to assess their performance against the average and to judge their relative position within the group.

The following are some examples of the ratios included in the BFMP scheme:

1. Operating Profit/Operating Capital
2. Operating Profit/Net Sales
3. Value of Output/Net Sales
4. Production Cost (Gross)/Cost of Output

* Lower quartile – ratio of the firm three-quarters down the list of ratings.

Median – ratio of the mid-point firm in the list of ratings.

Upper quartile – ratio of the firm one-quarter down the list of ratings.

168 FINANCE AND ACCOUNTS FOR MANAGERS

5. Distribution Cost/Cost of Output
6. Selling Cost/Cost of Output
7. Administration Cost/Cost of Output
8. Net Sales/Operating Capital
9. Fixed Assets/Operating Capital
10. Materials/Stock
11. Debtors/Sales per day
12. Value Added/Factory Employees
13. Value Added/Factory Wages

The fact that a firm shows an apparently unfavourable comparison under one or more of these ratio headings does not, of course, in itself necessarily mean that it is inefficient or wasteful in this particular respect. At best, it can only highlight the position for the management to note and to draw its own conclusions. In the case of a firm in the printing industry, it might be that it has taken a conscious policy decision to specialize in design work and as a result it employs a significantly higher than average number of artists and designers on its staff – this in expectation that its reputation for quality work will thereby be enhanced, and hence its ability to 'trade up' into a higher class of work and thus improve its ultimate competitive position.

Similarly, a firm which shows a higher than average ratio of fixed assets to capital employed may merely be reflecting the fact that it has had to resort to a higher degree of automation in its production processes so as to overcome local shortages of labour suited to its operating requirements. Such a policy might well result in a higher break even point, but provided that a sufficiently high level of plant utilization is achieved this may not be a serious drawback.

Ultimately, of course, any fundamental inefficiencies

will be reflected in the rate of return earned on capital employed and any deterioration in this ratio would require stringent examination, such scrutiny including a series of checks based on the principal ratios which provide the basis of these inter-firm schemes.

CHAPTER TWENTY-ONE

Taxation

The system of taxing business profits in the United Kingdom has become increasingly complex during recent years and in the case of limited companies considerable changes were brought about by the introduction of the Corporation Tax in the Finance Act 1965. However, the task of interpreting this voluminous legislation has been eased by the passing of the Income and Corporation Taxes Act 1970 and the Taxes Management Act 1970 which consolidate the succession of annual Finance Acts of the previous eighteen years.

Although those managers who do not have direct responsibility for the preparation of their company's annual accounts will not normally need to familiarize themselves with the detailed complexities of taxation law and practice, they will be better able to appreciate the broad background of business finance if they have some understanding of the basic structure of company taxation and the related capital investment incentive schemes.

The rate of Corporation Tax is determined by Parliament when it passes the annual Finance Acts and it is currently levied at 45 per cent. In addition, there is a charge for Income Tax (currently at 41·25 per cent) assessable on individual shareholders in respect of dividends paid to them out of these taxed profits. The following simple example illustrates the incidence of taxation on a company with earnings of £100,000 paying a

dividend of 10 per cent on its share capital of 500,000
£1 Ordinary Shares:

	£
Trading profit	100,000
Corporation Tax at 45 per cent	45,000
Profit after tax	55,000
Dividend on Ordinary Share capital	50,000
Net profit retained on business	£5,000

The shareholders will be assessed individually to Income
Tax at 41·25 per cent on the dividend of £50,000 – ie, a
total of £20,625.

The rate of Corporation Tax is determined in respect
of a 'financial year', being a year which commences on
1st April and ends on 31st March in the following cal-
endar year. Thus the 'financial year 1971' would be the
year commencing on April 1st, 1971, and ending on
March, 31st, 1972.

Since the passing of the Finance Act 1965, capital
profits have been subject to Corporation Tax in the
same way as normal trading profits.

The charge made in the accounts for depreciation of
capital assets is not an allowable expense for the purpose
of determining taxable profits and instead there is sub-
stituted a comprehensive range of 'capital allowances'
relating to plant, machinery, industrial buildings,
patents, research and development expenditure and
other defined expenditures of a capital nature. However, this system has been partially modified by the
introduction of Investment Grants under the Industrial
Development Act 1966, and certain categories of plant
and machinery now qualify for these outright cash grants

instead of capital allowances which operate by abating the tax charge.

The current rate for Investment Grants is 20 per cent but this is increased to 40 per cent for plant and machinery which is installed in certain specified geographical development areas. Capital equipment which does not qualify for these grants may nevertheless be eligible for the normal capital allowances, although certain types of expenditure are excluded altogether.

The system of grants and allowances for capital expenditure on plant, machinery, buildings and other equipment has been subject to many changes since the Second World War as succeeding governments have sought to regulate capital spending by industry in their attempts to control the national economy. Unfortunately, this constant uncertainty about the future of investment incentives has made many companies sceptical of relying on them as a factor in making their investment decisions and there has been a tendency to ignore their potential benefit when preparing and deciding on long-term capital expenditure projects.

There are, of course, a number of special grant schemes in existence designed to meet the needs of particular industries but they are outside the scope of this general summary of company taxation and capital incentive schemes.

The Finance Act 1965 introduced a special category of 'close company' which embraces most family businesses that are carried on as limited liability companies. These companies are subject to special provisions of a restrictive nature, particularly in regard to the taxation of undistributed profits, although recent Government fiscal policies have tended to modify some of the harsher aspects of this legislation as the contribution made by many smaller companies to the national economy has become more widely recognized.

Although taxation may sometimes appear to be an abstruse and remote subject to many managers, it is important for them to recognize that many apparently purely commercial decisions, particularly in regard to capital expenditure and the location of plants, can have significant fiscal implications which require close scrutiny by a competent tax expert and this should always be borne in mind before irrevocable commitments are entered into. This aspect of financial planning is of special importance for companies which form part of a group structure or where the possibility arises of opening plants in overseas territories. Indeed, tax planning has now taken its place alongside the many other specialisms that go to make up the corpus of management knowledge.

CHAPTER TWENTY-TWO

Capital for Expansion

The capital market in the United Kingdom comprises a highly complex structure of financial institutions which between them provide access to sources of capital for most sectors of industry and commerce.

A number of these institutions have been created to fulfil specialist roles; the Ship Mortgage Finance Co., Ltd, which was formed to assist British shipowners by providing finance for the construction of ships built in United Kingdom shipyards is a typical example, but in this chapter we are concerned only with those organizations which aim to provide finance for the wider range of businesses and for the wider range of requirements.

However, within this broad spectrum of financial institutions there is a high degree of specialization according to the purpose for which funds are required. Thus, a firm that is undergoing a phase of modest expansion which places a strain on its existing working capital resources would probably be well advised to turn in the first instance to its bankers to meet its requirements.

The joint stock banks regard their primary lending function to be that of providing capital on a strictly short term basis. This is not to say, of course, that banks will lend money only for short term financing; many companies rely on their bankers to provide regular access to funds to cover their working capital requirements during those periods when money is temporarily tied up in stocks and debtors. Nevertheless, such bank lendings are offered on the basis that the borrower undertakes to repay any loans on demand, and although in many instances such a request could not be met without causing the customer considerable embarrassment, the position is clearly established that there is no long term permanency about bank lending. Indeed, during periods of Government-induced 'credit squeezes', many bank managers do put strong pressure on some of their customers in an attempt to persuade them to repay their loans.

For companies that find the borrowing facilities available from their bankers to be insufficient to provide the necessary margin of working capital resources, there is the alternative possibility of factoring all or a part of their book debts. This type of financing operation entails assigning customers' accounts to a factoring house which will offer immediate cash subject to an appropriate rate of discount. The factoring house will then collect the cash proceeds as the debts become due for payment by the customers and, depending on the terms of the arrangement, possibly assuming the resulting credit risks. By using such a service the client company is able to convert its book debts into immediate cash rather than await the elapse of the normal period of delay which is entailed when financing its own customer credit.

Factoring operations of this nature are, when carried out by reputable finance houses, quite distinct from the activities carried on by debt-collecting agencies and they should not be confused with each other.

Companies engaged in the export trade that have difficulty in financing the extended commitment of working capital resources that is usually entailed may find some advantage in discounting the bills of exchange which are commonly used as a method of obtaining payment.* Bills of exchange are used to a lesser extent in the home market and where this is the practice they can, of course, be discounted in the same way. As with factoring, bill discounting is the function of specialist finance houses dealing with this type of business.

For the smaller companies that have not got ready access to the capital market, the financing of capital expenditure on new projects can be a serious problem. Without a large cash flow to provide a quick build up of funds from which to finance their commitments, their attempts to expand may be frustrated by the threatened diminution of their working capital resources which would result from over-ambitious spending on capital projects.

In these circumstances the most readily-available solution to the problem is for them to consider hire purchase or leasing of the capital assets which they are seeking to acquire. The latter form of finance is becoming increasingly widely accepted among industrialists and has the advantage that the leasing contract does not normally require a large initial deposit. Leasing finance companies cover a wide range of industries and requirements, with some specializing in particular fields such as office furniture and equipment and others extending their facilities to include such substantial assets as aircraft and heavy road haulage vehicles.

From the financial viewpoint, hire purchase and leas-

---

* Bills of exchange are negotiable instruments having similar characteristics to a cheque. They are drawn on the payer who becomes liable to meet the bill on acceptance; possibly at sight but often at a term of 30, 60 or 90 days after sight. In the export trade the acceptor cannot obtain documents of title to the goods (bills of lading, etc) until the bill has been accepted.

ing contracts entail the acceptance of a fixed regular commitment on cash resources which must be met each month regardless of the trading position, but for many companies this is more than outweighed by the avoidance of a heavy drain on their cash funds at a time when their working capital resources are possibly fully committed in other directions.

Companies that are planning to expand on a broadly based development programme which entails a larger financing problem than can be solved by any of the methods discussed above will have to consider a more radical approach. In the case of non-quoted companies, ie those which cannot readily seek funds from the wider investing public, the sources to which they might turn for large amounts of capital are severely restricted. One of the best known organizations which exists for the purpose of providing finance for the smaller companies is the Industrial and Commercial Finance Corporation Ltd. Set up in 1945 by the Bank of England in conjunction with the principal English and Scottish clearing banks, it has been the financial foster-parent to a number of thriving businesses which have progressed to major status with the aid of its resources. A large proportion of its lending is in the form of loan capital over periods of from ten to twenty years and applicants are closely vetted from every angle before they are accepted.

However, within the broad band of companies that is within ICFC's prospective range of interest the demand for capital is considerably larger than the supply and consequently some good prospects are deterred from making even the preliminary approaches.

Among other organizations which consider investing in some of the more efficient smaller companies are the

Charterhouse Group and Estate Duties Investment Trust Ltd.

The Finance Corporation for Industry (FCI) is another financial institution which, sponsored by the Bank of England in conjunction with insurance companies and investment trusts, exists to provide backing to a selected range of industrial companies. It aims at a rather larger size of company than the ICFC and the amounts advanced tend to be similarly scaled up.

Some of the larger superannuation funds which have large inflows of funds requiring regular investment are a major factor in the business world and they have occasionally shown signs of being interested in investing in some of the medium-small companies which show signs of being potential 'high-fliers'. However, this is not an important source of funds at the present time and the opportunities for raising capital in this way are not significant.

Once a company reaches the stage when it can consider the transition to public company status it has considerably widened the range of opportunities open to it for raising new capital. By obtaining a quotation on a recognized stock exchange (either the London Stock Exchange or one or more of the provincial exchanges) it can seek to raise capital by the issue of a prospectus inviting applications for its securities from the public.

However, it is not within the scope of this volume to consider the detailed procedures by which capital issues are made but rather to appreciate the broader outlines of the problems of raising business capital.

For the public company one of the major considerations which inevitably influence the timing of an issue of permanent capital is the prevailing rate of interest as set by Bank Rate and reflected in the yields obtainable from various types of securities. It would be unwise to make an issue of permanent capital at a time when Bank Rate is at an abnormally high level, thus placing a premium on the terms of issue which will thereafter be a permanent burden on annual trading profits. In these circumstances it would be advisable to rely on short term finance until conditions have improved and the cost of long term borrowing has fallen to a more acceptable level.

Many smaller companies, particularly those whose shares are not quoted on a recognized stock exchange, rely on retained earnings to provide them with funds for expansion, but the accumulation of capital in this way is a slow process which in all probability does little more than provide a minimum level of funds to carry out essential replacements of fixed assets. For companies that have to conserve their cash resources in this way, they will need to restrict their spending on fixed capital assets to their anticipated cash flow. The cash flow is the company's net trading profits after taxation and dividends, plus the amount provided for depreciation of fixed assets, viz:

	£
Trading profit for year	50,000
(after providing £20,000 for depreciation of fixed assets)	
Corporation Tax	20,000
	30,000
Dividend	15,000
Net retained profits	£15,000

Cash Flow = Net retained profits £15,000
Plus depreciation £20,000 = £35,000

Thus, the new cash generated by the company is represented by the retained profits and the cash retentions arising from the sums set aside for depreciation of fixed assets.

Companies that own the freeholds of their premises could well consider the possibility of selling them off to a property company and leasing them back under a long term lease. By negotiating an arrangement of this nature they are able to free capital resources which are tied up in the form of land and buildings and turn them to alternative uses in carrying on their business. It follows, of course, that there will be an additional annual charge against profits in respect of the rent which would henceforth be payable and the financial justification for such an operation must rest on the company being able to employ the capital resources in their new activity at a rate of return that is significantly greater than this extra cost.

A not unimportant source of access to capital for some smaller companies is that which can be obtained by aligning themselves with one of the industrial holding company groups that have come into prominence within recent years. The Thomas Tilling Group of Companies is probably one of the best known of this type of organization but there are a number of others (the Norcros Group is another prominent example) and they frequently invite suitable companies with good growth prospects to apply to be brought into the group. Such take-overs are often the outcome of amicable negotiations, with the existing management being invited to stay and help run the company under its new ownership. By joining one of these industrial groupings a smaller company can avail itself of the facilities and resources of a larger financial group without necessarily sacrificing all its independence of action in the pursuit of its trading objectives.

These industrial holding companies are in some respects more akin to investment companies, particularly when they retain the subsidiary company managements and spread their interests across a broad range of industries. By way of contrast, such large industrial groups as ICI, Courtaulds, the Rank Organization, and similar organizations tend, in spite of the disparate nature of some of their activities, to be run as fairly closely-knit and tightly-managed entities with the main board directing overall policy in fairly specific terms.

Index

MANAGEMENT SERIES

MANAGEMENT DECISION MAKING 30p
A symposium of five international experts – British and American – stress the importance of scientific decision making in modern business administration.

MARKETING MANAGEMENT IN ACTION 60p
Victor P. Buell. A guide to successful marketing management by a former national vice-president of the American Marketing Association.

THE PRACTICE OF MANAGEMENT 50p
Peter F. Drucker. An outstanding contribution to management theory and practice.

MANAGING FOR RESULTS 40p
Peter F. Drucker. A what to do book for the top echelons of management.

THE EFFECTIVE EXECUTIVE 35p
Peter F. Drucker. How to develop the five talents essential to effectiveness and mould them into results by practical decision-making.

THE AGE OF DISCONTINUITY 60p
Peter F. Drucker. The author presents numerous practical examples from Central Europe, Britain, US and Japan to produce 'A major work of great brilliance . . . eminently'.

CYBERNETICS IN MANAGEMENT 40p
F. H. George. Introduction to the ideas and methods used by cyberneticians in the running of modern business and government.

PLANNED MARKETING 30p
Ralph Glasser. A lucid introduction to mid-Atlantic marketing techniques.

INNOVATION IN MARKETING 37½p
Theodore Levitt. A brilliant exposition of original and stimulating ideas on modern approaches to marketing.

MANAGEMENT SERIES (cont.)

THE ESSENCE OF PRODUCTION 40p
P. H. Lowe. Explains the components, diversities and problems of production within the general framework of business management.

MAKING MANPOWER EFFECTIVE Part 1 37½p
James J. Lynch. The techniques of company manpower planning and forecasting.

A MANPOWER DEVELOPMENT SYSTEM 40p
Part 2 of MAKING MANPOWER EFFECTIVE. Shows the need to integrate manpower forecasting, compensation planning and career development into a manpower development system.

CAREERS IN MARKETING 30p
An Institute of Marketing Review. A guide to those seeking a job in the exciting field of marketing.

THE PROPERTY BOOM (illus.) 37½p
Oliver Marriott. The story of the personalities and the companies that emerged enriched from the commercial property industry in the years 1945–1965.

SELLING AND SALESMANSHIP 30p
R. G. Magnus-Hannaford. A clear, concise and forward looking exposition of practical principles and their application.

MARKETING 37½p
Colin McIver. Includes chapters by Gordon Wilson on the Years of Revolution and Industrial Marketing.

EXPORTING: A Basic Guide to Selling Abroad 37½p
Robin Neillands and Henry Deschampsneufs. Shows how smaller and medium-sized companies can effectively obtain and develop overseas markets.

DYNAMIC BUSINESS MANAGEMENT 30p
Harold Norcross. A simple guide to the rudiments of successful business management.

FINANCIAL PLANNING AND CONTROL 40p
R. E. Palmer and A. H. Taylor. Explains the nature of the assistance which levels of accounting can provide in the planning and control of a modern business.

MANAGEMENT SERIES (cont.)

COMPUTERS FOR MANAGEMENT 30p
Peter C. Sanderson. A timely appraisal of computers and electronic data processing – their basic concepts, potential and business application.

GUIDE TO SAMPLING 30p
Morris James Slonim. A fine exposition of sampling theory and techniques.

MANAGEMENT INFORMATION –
Its Computation and Communication 40p
C. W. Smith, G. P. Mead, C. T. Wicks and G. A. Yewdall. Discusses Education in Business Management, Statistics for Business, Mathematics and Computing, Operational Research, Communicating Numerical Data.

MANAGERS AND THEIR JOBS 35p
Rosemary Stewart. Helps managers to analyse what they can do, why they do it, and whether they can, in fact, do it better.

THE REALITY OF MANAGEMENT 35p
Rosemary Stewart. Compass bearings to help the manager plot his career.

HOW TO WIN CUSTOMERS 45p
Heinz M. Goldmann. A leading European sales consultant with unique experience of British, Canadian, US and European markets examines the sixteen areas of creative selling.

These Management Series titles are obtainable from all booksellers and newsagents. If you have any difficulty please send purchase price plus 5p postage to Claude Gill Books, 481 Oxford Street, London, W.1, where the whole series is on display.

While every effort is made to keep prices low, it is sometimes necessary to increase prices at short notice. PAN Books reserve the right to show new retail prices on covers which may differ from those previously advertised in the text or elsewhere.

THE MONEY GAME
ADAM SMITH 35p

Internationally acclaimed – The American bestseller which 'writes about money with the infectious excitement of a crime story. What is money, who makes it, and how? THE SUNDAY TIMES

'Fascinating, the funniest book on investment I have ever read but it is also packed with wisdom' SUNDAY MIRROR

'For amusement, insight and readability I don't know a better book, on or off the Stock Exchange's approved reading list ... If you are interested in money – and who isn't? – you, regardless of sex, should buy a copy' THE DAILY TELEGRAPH

THE PETER PRINCIPLE 30p
DR. LAURENCE J. PETER & RAYMOND HULL

'Have you ever wondered how that bunch of idiots got control of your office/shop/factory? ... The answer is supplied in **The Peter Principle**' – DAILY MIRROR

'Will be read by millions wanting to diagnose what is wrong with their colleagues' – SUNDAY TELEGRAPH

'Just enough truth behind it all to be rather disturbing' – DAILY EXPRESS

A SELECTION OF POPULAR READING IN PAN

FICTION

ROYAL FLASH	George MacDonald Fraser	30p
THE FAME GAME	Rona Jaffe	40p
SILENCE ON MONTE SOLE	Jack Olsen	35p
A TASTE OF DEATH	Peter O'Donnell	30p
TRAMP IN ARMOUR	Colin Forbes	30p
SHOTGUN	Ed McBain	25p
EMBASSY	Stephen Coulter	30p
AIRPORT	Arthur Hailey	37½p
HEIR TO FALCONHURST	Lance Horner	40p
REQUIEM FOR A WREN	Nevil Shute	30p
MADAME SERPENT	Jean Plaidy	30p
MURDER MOST ROYAL	Jean Plaidy	35p
CATHERINE	Juliette Benzoni	35p

NON-FICTION

THE SOMERSET & DORSET RAILWAY (illus.)	Robbin Atthill	35p
THE WEST HIGHLAND RAILWAY (illus.)	John Thomas	35p
MY BEAVER COLONY (illus.)	Lars Wilsson	25p
THE SMALL GARDEN (illus.)	C. E. Lucas-Phillips	40p
HOW TO WIN CUSTOMERS	Heinz M. Goldmann	45p
THE NINE BAD SHOTS OF GOLF (illus.)	Jim Dante & Leo Diegel	35p

These and other advertised PAN Books are obtainable from all booksellers and newsagents. If you have any difficulty please send purchase price plus 5p postage to P.O. Box 11, Falmouth, Cornwall. While every effort is made to keep prices low it is sometimes necessary to increase prices at short notice. PAN Books reserve the right to show new retail prices on covers which may differ from those advertised in the text or elsewhere.